The Emergence of Us

The Emergence of Us

Tim Gooding

iUniverse, Inc.
New York Lincoln Shanghai

The Emergence of Us

iUniverse books may be ordered through booksellers or by contacting:

iUniverse
2021 Pine Lake Road, Suite 100
Lincoln, NE 68512
www.iuniverse.com
1-800-Authors (1-800-288-4677)

ISBN-13: 978-0-595-40653-1 (pbk)
ISBN-13: 978-0-595-85019-8 (ebk)
ISBN-10: 0-595-40653-X (pbk)
ISBN-10: 0-595-85019-7 (ebk)

Printed in the United States of America

Contents

Acknowledgements

This book is the culmination of over twenty years of work, so if I were to name names, the list would be longer than the book itself. Every person that has been in my life has added to this book in some way, and though none were directly involved in its actual creation, they all live within these pages.

However, the cover only took a few weeks. The original concept came from Juliet Holding and Ben Pike from Larger Pix in the UK had the vision to make it come to life.

Cheerful Street Cleaners

If we look at ourselves honestly, what many of us really want is to be handed a solution to society's problems, such as global warming, that does not force changes into our lives. Of course this seems ideal, but it is very unlikely. The state of the world is a direct expression of the way we all live in it right now.

Resistance to change is natural, especially if you like the life you have. But what if it can be demonstrated that there exists a considerably better possibility for you, even if you count among the richest and most powerful in the world today?

Sometimes, even cheerful street cleaners can wish for a different way to express their potential. The journey to this expression will certainly entail change. Some free time might be lost to study, or pub money might be diverted to training. Perhaps the change is significant and all resources are mobilized. The street cleaner identification completely vanishes and is replaced by something like a student, disciple, or explorer.

It is common sense that we can accomplish very little if we refuse to change. The trick is to find a way to change that will create the potential for a better life than is possible now.

This book is about the recognition and mastery of forces that have largely remained invisible and yet continue herd the behavior and thoughts of all of us. In order to step outside these forces and regain our potential, we are going to have to be willing to change. Sometimes, we may have to give up things that immediately give us pleasure in order to bring into existence something far more profoundly satisfying for us and generations that follow.

These forces emerge as soon as a critical number of people is passed. Human emergent behavior forms and begins the process of defining the rationale for thoughts and deeds, in effect usurping the control of any group. Frequently, local rationality and global rationality becomes disconnected.

For example, generating greenhouse gases is irrational if global warming is a concern. However, our society is shaped so that a powerful local rationale exists for people to repeatedly make the choice to pollute. Today, waves of third world people are racing to become equal partners in the pollution of the earth. Reshaping these forces could enable us to create waves of people racing to live cleanly, all the while living a better life that can be achieved today in any country.

By learning to recognize and direct these forces, we could effectively dissolve a number of societal problems that are currently considered an unavoidable part of life. Our transition could be remarkably painless if we are aware of what we are doing and where we are going.

If we can agree that personal change might be necessary, and possibly even desirable, then we have already reached the first step. The rest of this book is about understanding what is happening to us, and developing the awareness necessary to bring a loving consciousness to the great domineering presence that is human emergent behavior.

The Principle of Many Things

Our Peak

Because of the nature of our current emergent system, society resides on a peak that is characterized by a relentless drive towards economic efficiency and continued technological advancements. While this creates a constant stream of improvements in our ability to generate invention and wealth, the quality of human experience is not necessarily directly tied to either. There exists an instinctive yearning for a society that holds people as its priority instead of economic wealth and invention.

A few decades ago, oil was discovered on Native American land in Canada. The deal to extract it gave every man, woman, and child of that tribe $40,000 per year for every year the operations were taking place. At the time, $40,000 was a very good annual wage indeed. A family of four earned $120,000 per year—an executive level income in those days. They instantly exchanged a life of poverty for one of easy wealth. If money makes people happy, then that tribe would have burst with joy. In fact, the suicide rate went up several times higher than the average of all other Native American communities in Canada, many of which were still struggling with intense poverty and severe social problems.

This is only one example supporting a growing body of research showing that once our basic needs are fulfilled, more wealth does not make much difference to our happiness. One must wonder what might be possible if the substantial energies currently spent generating wealth were redirected to something directly linked to human happiness.

There are many peaks possible for humankind and this economic/technological peak is unlikely to be either the highest or the best. But moving from one peak to another is a tricky business. The incentive to stay on whatever peak we happen to find ourselves on is very strong, even if the surrounding peaks are obviously much higher.

The base of all peaks contain within them incentives to stay the course on that particular slope and climb to the top. If people unknowingly climb onto the first

1

base they find, they can find themselves trapped on any number of random peaks, some of which can be ultimately destructive.

For a drug addict, the base of that peak is their first high and the experience of repeated highs is the peak. To come off drugs, not only must the addict give up the repeated highs, but he must also be prepared to go through a rather painful detoxification. All bad. Since any of these moves will immediately bring about a less pleasant existence for an addict, what rational reason does an addict have to come off the peak?

Of course, it is easy for outside observers to recognize the higher peaks of possibility surrounding the addict. Not only that, but we know that an addict will adapt to the highs, making it progressively more difficult to maintain the same level. The potential satisfaction from being on this peak is reducing over time. That means the entire peak is falling. If the drug is sufficiently destructive, the peak might collapse all the way to death.

The only way to bring about a rational desire to come off the addiction peak is for the addict to gain a greater awareness of the situation. Using immediate gratification to determine action will doom anyone to remain on the first peak they find, no matter how it measures up to their larger surroundings. If the addict becomes aware of larger possibilities, it is much easier to generate the willpower necessary to get off their falling peak and find a new base. Unfortunately, the facts necessary for the addict to fully understand the situation are frequently very hard to hear. The reaction can easily be denial. Too much denial will make this path unworkable.

Our society resides on an economic/technological peak that is sinking. Every moment we stay on it, we lose ground. All our instincts are to cling to the top, trusting that the system that has given us so much will once again save us from an outcome that many predict will be rather unpleasant.

As a whole, humankind wields an enormous unconscious power. We have even changed the direction of the earth's weather system, a vast complex natural system that dwarfs the abilities of our technologies. Try to imagine the magnitude of this accomplishment if global warming had been our conscious goal. If we can accomplish something as large as this by accident, with no effort or planning, what might be possible if we could consciously direct these forces?

As things are now, our power is so unconscious that when global warming was first detected, many people refused to believe we were involved at all. This is not necessarily because they were evil or stupid, but because they instinctively realized what it would really mean. Without conscious access to the power that created the problem in the first place, we are left with only very expensive and weak devices to combat it. Using only the tools found on our economic/technological peak, making the profound and immediate changes that would be necessary to contain the problem of global warming would cripple the world's economy. This would not just involve the loss of profits, but could precipitate serious problems such as (more) starvation. We might even be forced off our current peak and left to tumble into whatever valley happens to be waiting for us.

Part of our tendency towards inaction comes from a feeling that somehow society "out there" will not only find ways to combat global warming, but it will protect us if it does occur. As powerful as our society is, in some ways it is very vulnerable. Cause and effect in a system as large as humankind is not always what it seems. For example, many people claim that there is clean energy, like solar power, available right now. They suggest that we might switch from fossil fuels to these new clean energies. Like so many things in life, it is not a simple as this.

Consequences can change dramatically as any local presence goes global, because the character of an emergent system changes with numbers. What started out clean on a small scale can become a dirty nightmare on a larger scale, and visa versa.

When the automobile was first introduced in London, it was celebrated for its cleanliness because no longer did thousands of tons of horse manure need to be cleaned off London streets every single day. These huge growing manure piles were becoming a blight on the landscape for everyone in the area and were requiring the dedication of thousands of workers to maintain them. If nothing had changed, the world would have an unbelievable manure problem today.

The introduction of the automobile to London streets completely solved the problem. It was immediately obvious to everyone in London that automobiles were much cleaner and more hygienic than horses. So, is it not logical that flooding the world with cars would make the world a safe clean place?

There are now voices in society trying to recreate this scenario with nuclear power. The argument is that nuclear power is a powerful way to create energy without creating greenhouse gases. This is true. However, nuclear waste damages and destroys DNA whenever the two of them come within close proximity. DNA is the one thing necessary to all known life. Consciously deciding to create even limited amounts of a waste product this dangerous to all known life seems suspect to me. If countries embrace nuclear power as the standard means to produce power, nuclear waste will be created on an industrial scale. To me, this looks like it could be the seed for another global crisis, and one that could dwarf global warming in its impact.

All emergent systems exhibit character changes as numbers pass critical points. Many people see the higher peaks around us and endeavor to explain how we can move over to this new place one person at a time. Unfortunately, what might be wonderful for one person or group can turn into something completely different when implemented globally. There are many sustainable food or energy systems being promoted as "green". Locally, they work fantastically, but if they were to be implemented on a global level we might find ourselves simply exchanging one global threat for another.

If this were to happen, who should we blame? As the death and damage from the shifting climate mounts, some people naturally want to find the villains so we can apply some justice. But what would we do if it turns out that all the people and organizations that we thought were the problem were just as powerless as the rest of us? What if it turns out there are no villains?

Most of us have a passing knowledge of which activities cause damage and yet everyday we choose to engage in these very activities that are collectively threatening the stability of the world climate. There is probably not one person reading this that did not contribute to global warming today.

As many have been telling us for so long, perhaps we all simply have to behave in a different way in order to save our environment. Well, that is fine, but how? Did you pollute the environment today? Did you listen to music or watch television, eat food not grown by yourself, travel anywhere (including by bicycle), wear clothes not grown and made by yourself? If the answer is yes to any of these questions, plus many more, then you, personally, directly contributed to earth pollution today.

Right now, I am writing on a laptop made of plastic (oil) and heavy metals (toxic to carbon life forms), consuming electricity (coal, oil, nuclear) sitting in a warm house during winter being heated by gas (oil drilling, greenhouse gases). All this polluting was perpetrated in just a few minutes of me sitting on the couch. I'm likely to eat some cereal soon…let's not even go there.

If you and I are not willing to change today, right now, then what is going to make you and me willing to change in the next hour? Tomorrow? Next year? Next lifetime?

Now imagine this; society subtly changes. You no longer have to think about pollution. In fact, it becomes necessary for you to make an effort if you want to create, for example, a greenhouse gas. If everyone had to spend money and time every time they wanted to create greenhouse gas, what chance does greenhouse gas have?

Sounds like a fantasy, doesn't it? However, as everyone becomes more aware of the forces we are going to explore and how they work, it not only becomes possible, but likely.

Our Lenses

After the tsunami that hit Indonesia in 2004, some people were concerned about the fate of the Jarawa. They are the last 300 people of an isolated tribe living their traditional life on tiny islands that lay in the direct path of that deadly tsunami. Their shoreline villages were undoubtedly destroyed.

They did not have any understanding of the science of tectonic plates, earthquakes or the resulting waves. They had no hospitals to care for the injured. They had no central government or charities to dispatch assistance. They did not have any television or radio to tell them what was going on in the world outside their little island. They do not recognize the Christian/Muslim/Jehovah God so even miracles were not on offer.

All the Jarawa had was an old spiritual belief featuring various spirits with different personalities striding their world. For many modern people, this belief system is simply a primitive and simplistic picture of the world. What could possibly be lost if this belief system disappeared to be replaced by a more modern understanding of the world?

As soon as it became possible a helicopter was dispatched to find out how best to help. When it arrived it was discovered that not one single person from these primitive tribes had been killed or injured.

Of course, the question had to be asked; why not?

A tribesman answered that his people's understanding of spirits indicated that the land spirit and the sea spirit were about to fight over territory. When the water line began to shift outside normal tidal movements, the people immediately knew that a battle was imminent. The spirits' wrath can be terrible to behold, so the people ran for the hills. This fight was a bad one and many homes were destroyed in the spirits' fight, but none of the Jarawa was even injured. Life returned to normal within hours after the tsunami.

The Jarawa's primitive pagan belief system saved their lives. If everyone in Indonesia has held these same beliefs, the tsunami would have killed very few people or, perhaps, no one at all. On the other hand, if we had converted the Jarawa to either our modern scientific or religious beliefs, many of them would now be dead.

Their belief system is not superior to yours or mine. However, it did contain life-saving information about events that were beyond the Jarawa's ability to understand. For their environment and lifestyle, their belief system is custom tailored to help them survive and thrive far more successfully, as it turned out, than other apparently more sophisticated and accurate belief systems surrounding them.

The greatest gift of all the religions and spiritual belief systems is that they can encompass wisdom that resides outside our current ability to comprehend. As with the Jarawa, this can include practical life-saving information that is not readily accessible even to people with our most modern understandings of the real world.

No belief system, whether science based or spiritual/faith based, contains all the information of reality. In spite of our great joy of constructing models to represent reality, the shortest expression of reality is reality itself. There are no shortcuts. All the information present in any moment of reality is so far beyond our ability to obtain, retain, or even comprehend, that the best we can do is decide what information to grasp and let the rest fall away.

The tool we use to determine what information is important enough to grasp is our beliefs, whether they are formalized institutional beliefs or an unconscious private little belief held only by you. Once in place, our belief automatically filters out irrelevant information and provides a framework for interpreting the information we have judged to be important. Every belief in the world works as a specialized lens on reality.

People choose to look through microscopes because they powerfully focus on a specific part of our world. Without them, an entire area of reality would still be a mystery to us. The same could be said of telescopes.

While each of these lenses gifts us with information that is otherwise unobtainable, there is a trade-off. As we concentrate on the revelations of one lens, the rest of the world passes by unnoticed. Anyone would be horrified at the thought of being forced to only look through one lens all their life, regardless of their level of interest. They would miss so much!

But this creates a problem. Any time we are not looking through the revealing lens of the microscope, for example, we are missing information coming from that part of reality. Whether we watch it or not, it will continue to change and develop, possibly moving towards something that can re-write history. Reality happens whether we are looking or not. In 1918, the bird flu virus took the world completely by surprise and killed over 50,000,000 people. The shock to society was so great that some people think it was the most influential factor causing the end of World War I.

At the time, no one was looking at viruses and so anything going on in that reality was invisible to all of society. Luckily for us, we now have thousands of different people constantly looking through all sorts of lenses and reporting to society as a whole. As a result, we are aware of a picture that is far greater than any one person could possibly perceive alone.

This seems quite obvious. So then why don't we do the same thing with our belief lenses?

It would be an enormous gift to all of us if we all could report from our lens to the awareness of society as a whole. If, by some unfortunate series of events, we all started seeing through the same belief system, we would become blind to whole sections of reality. One of humankind's greatest potentials resides in the fact that we all perceive things differently.

Unfortunately, while no one gets overly upset over whether we look in microscopes or telescopes, life's lenses tend to make people a bit more trigger happy. In our world today, people are routinely killed for not seeing life through the favorite lens of the killer. This is one of the saddest habits of humanity. On a daily basis, many people tear apart the delicate fabric of one of our greatest possibilities.

Unlike the microscope and telescope, people have huge emotional investments in the lens they use for life. Even people who believe they are very open-minded will unconsciously lock the gates to possibility whenever they feel challenged on long past decisions made about reality.

This is a natural characteristic that emerges from all successful belief systems, but it is something that must be examined carefully. There is a treasure to be had if we can find the courage to occasionally look outside the accepted walls of our favorite lens to explore the wisdom revealed by other lenses.

If all of humankind did this, an amazing thing would happen. We could link up all the different belief lenses in a way that would include everyone. The vision we would have is indescribable in the face of our current experience. It would be a leap of understanding and experience far beyond the comprehension of any lone belief system, regardless of how profound the residing wisdom is in any one belief.

Sometimes we may think that what we see through our respective lenses completely contradicts one another, but wherever our lens contains truth then there will be a meeting place somewhere in reality. It may not be evident at first glance, the same way that the picture seen in a microscope is quite different from what is seen in a telescope. However, finding these meeting places is well worth the effort.

As we approach a place where all lenses meet, more and more beliefs will need to be validated and we will likely be challenged right to the edge of our ability. At the center, the truth of all lenses must be equally valid. By allowing the validity of all our beliefs to be present an enormous human potential could be realized.

Where all our beliefs meet in reality are staging points. No matter the differences, everyone agrees that gravity affects us right now. It doesn't matter whether it is God's hand, the denseness of belief, or mass in space/time; gravity will make things fall. A scientific, spiritual or theological argument is not required to know that if the wings have just fallen off your airplane then you are going down.

But as soon as we drift off this staging point everything diverges. The scientists among us will tell us that it is a force resulting from mass existing in space/time continuum. Some spiritualists will say that it is an illusion to be overcome. The religious might suggest that it is the hand of God, for He/She/It is omnipotent. And then we fight and fight and fight over who is right.

For those of us who want to peer through lenses other than our own, we can use these meeting places as a staging point to trek out to other lenses and beliefs. In the first two sections I am going to try to stick as close to staging points as possible. Even if it seems I have gone off the deep end, if you examine the terrain carefully with an open mind, you will probably find a staging area quite close by.

Once we strip away the need to be philosophically right, several issues can quickly become clear. For example, let's look at how we are affecting the weather. What is happening is that carbon dioxide is accumulating within our atmosphere. It doesn't matter whether it is the result of sin, evil spirits, or industrialization (did you just dismiss the beliefs that you felt were ridiculous?). Carbon dioxide traps heat from the sun, so more carbon dioxide in the atmosphere will increase the energy in our weather system. Whether the sun is also heating us up or not does not alter the fact that our actions are affecting our weather.

How these new energy levels are going to express themselves is unknown, regardless of what experts tell us. There are doubtless some very good guesses (there are so many that one is bound to be right), but the weather system contains numerous feedback systems making it possible for even the tiniest initial inputs to create radical long-term consequences. There are uncountable tiny new variations being spun out by the accumulating energy, all of which will affect the overall expression of our weather.

Another fact is that even though we intellectually know how to stop global warming, world wide we are only making token moves. In other words, in spite of a possible mortal danger to ourselves, we aren't really doing anything about it. There are those who argue that humankind is not acting rationally if life is the goal. But if individuals are making rational decisions that result in global warming, then in order to use command to change society we would have to compel people to act irrationally. This leads to a very bad place. It might be better to reconnect the rationality of individual behavior with that of rational global behavior.

All the different lenses have their specialties and we will be visiting a few of them. What we need now is a lens that is interested in what measurably happens in our reality. What are the seemingly immutable laws that all of us live by regardless of what we believe? Discovering and describing these laws is the purpose of the science lens.

One of the unique strengths of science is that it is one of the few beliefs where there is a reward for destroying its own carefully guarded sacred cows. It constantly searches for problems in its own truths. Individual scientists may get trapped into thinking that a theory is a fact, but science as a whole will quickly move past any "fact" if someone can prove that it is wrong. Sometimes there is an initial period of ridicule and derision, but science as a whole is just too curious to hold onto false truths in the face of contradictory evidence for too long.

This does not mean that the science lens has no weaknesses or that it is superior to other lenses. It is simply the place where we are starting this journey.

The Child of Simplicity

Some problems are simply too complex for us to solve using equations. Since the core of all the scientific disciplines concerns the creation of equations that successfully describe reality and therefore can predict and solve problems, this is a serious barrier to science understanding the real world. However, we have recently discovered a method to solve previously insurmountable problems.

What scientists and engineers have done is recreate real world problems in a computer environment, and then create thousands of simple random computer "beings" and set them against the problem. These "beings" have a set lifetime and those who make the most advancement against the problem are allowed to reproduce themselves. The engineers let everything run until several generations of little computer "beings" have come and gone and a solution emerges.

Danny Hillis, one of the people to experiment with these principles, discovered a fascinating thing (actually many fascinating things, but we'll start with one). After his programmed scenario had successfully learned to solve the problem that Hillis had set, he became naturally curious as to exactly how the emerged solution worked. Since it was a computer program, and all computer programs do is to instruct the computer one single step at a time, it would be easy. By following the steps in the final code, he could see how the program instructed the computer. And thus it was, except for one little problem. Hillis, a man with several University degrees, could not understand how the solution worked. In fact, he wondered if anyone would ever understand how the evolved program worked.

How could this be?

Let's start at the beginning. If we throw together random words hoping for a functioning sentence to appear the chances would not be very good. However, if we did it several million times, it is almost inevitable that a sentence would appear at some time. Another way of saying it is; given eternity, no matter how long the odds are, it is an absolute certainty that sentences will appear.

Computer code is simply a set of very simple sentences that instruct the computer. The most complex computer achievements, including artificial intelligence, all boil down to simple lines of instruction such as x equals whatever x was plus 1. If x was 3, after this instruction x becomes 4. It really is this simple.

So when Hillis decided to throw together random computer instructions looking for working computer programs, it does not seem so mad. In fact, if you do this enough times, it is inevitable that functioning computer programs will appear. However, instead of using time, Hillis used numbers. He simultaneously threw together computer code into thousands and thousands of different little computer programs. Of course, most of them were completely useless, but enough functioning programs appeared that he could move onto the next step.

He set loose all his newly created programs, functioning and non-functioning, into a computer environment that contained random numbers. What he wanted his little programs to accomplish was to order the numbers in as few steps as possible. Of course, his little accidentally-created programs had no such specific instruction. At first, they did very little indeed.

His environment was designed to give the little programs a limited time to operate before they died. Before they died, they would be permitted to reproduce themselves according to how successful they were in ordering numbers. The little programs that were better at ordering the numbers were allowed more offspring.

Using these principles, Hillis hoped that they would evolve to eventually order the numbers. He had no idea if it would take days, months, or even years. He threw the switch, so to speak.

A few minutes later, his programs were finished evolving and had solved the problem.

From a completely random set of computer code Hillis had evolved powerful number sorters with no planning at all. In fact, he didn't need to know anything about the problem. The only knowledge he needed was how to set up a system to evolve solutions. After that, the system did all the work for him.

But it didn't just solve the problem. Hillis was aware of the enormous potential of this kind of system, so he wasn't content simply to evolve number sorters. He was looking for a world record contender.

Ordering numbers is the computer programmer's version of the hundred meter sprint. Many people can run a hundred meters, but only the world's best can do it in under ten seconds. Hillis evolved a program that managed it in sixty two steps when the world record was sixty. Hillis' accomplishment is like an inactive office worker sitting on a couch thinking of how to sprint and then showing up at the Olympics and running a hundred meters in ten seconds flat.

So where did this powerful complexity come from? Certainly not from the problem. Ordering numbers isn't overly difficult, even for children. Can you imagine what solutions a system like this could create for problems that are too complex for us to understand?

Emergent systems have the capacity to utilize principles that are not normally consciously engaged in our everyday thinking. So, the solutions they generate are frequently outside our normal awareness. This process might look magical to some people, but it is no more "magical" than a light bulb or radio would have been to people a thousand years ago.

There are a couple of things that need to be emphasized for later consideration. One is that at no time was the number sorting goal ever programmed into the individual units. Individually, they had no idea of where they were going and never did. In fact, even if a group of them rose up and "protested" about becoming good number sorters, it would make no difference whatsoever to their inevitable destination. Hillis' entire system moved with irresistible force in a direction determined by a force outside the "lifetime" of the little programs.

In this particular case, the fact that the more successful number counters were best able to reproduce guided everything. Except for the ability to sort numbers, what an individual program achieved in its lifetime mattered not at all. Even if it evolved emotions and awareness, the only action that could change the outcome of this particular system is to change the reproductive preference. It would take an enormous evolutionary jump for the individual programs to become aware enough and powerful enough to reach out and change that parameter on their own accord. But that is the only available option for programs within to change their destiny. Nothing else they do as individuals, or even as groups, will make the slightest difference in the long-term.

The state of the initial code of the individual programmed units was also irrelevant. The more independent and varied the individual units are, the more powerful the overall system becomes because there is more for the system to work with to accomplish its prime directive. This is why Hillis could use random computer code. The ubiquitous force emerging from this system will channel all the little "beings" to their new form with invisible and irresistible power. The characteristics and tendencies of the individual units are all utilized to enable the overall system to best develop its final solution. It was their inevitable destiny because that was the imperative created by their emergent system.

One of the keys to the success of a system like this is to allow variation to occur. Looking at one program cycle (one life-time) we might notice that some programs seem completely useless. We could artificially remove the inefficient in the hope that leaving only the best programs would create a better problem-solving system. However, a system like this processes all the information within it, including that which seems to us to have no use whatsoever. It would make sense that if this system can evolve something outside our understanding then it is doing something that we don't normally accept as useful. In other words, if we try to intellectually improve upon the process of the system, there is a good chance we will simply reduce it to our level of thinking. The magic will disappear.

It turns out that using these principles we have solved all manner of previously unsolvable real world problems in various disciplines, including engineering, crowd control, and traffic management. Sometimes we might not be able to understand the solutions, so it is fortunate that all we had to do is implement them.

Can we agree that this is a profound way of thinking outside of the box?

The Great Flow

Whether they are allowed to express it or not, most people agree that free will does exist in people. The potential for any person to do anything at any time always exists. With all this free will surging in our veins, how is it ever possible to predict anything?

In crowded places across the world, a completely ordinary but magical thing regularly occurs. Because it is common, no one really thinks about it. Pausing for just a moment, however, reveals its extraordinary unlikelihood.

Can you picture a city pedestrian scene in your head? People with the free will to go at any speed they want—to go in any direction they want—to roll about on the ground if they like—to walk on their hands—with the ability to choose from an infinite number of possibilities at every given moment, in reality, consistently choose to walk up and down the pavement in relatively orderly flows. Given that they can choose from all of reality, the fact that millions of people from countries and cultures and beliefs all over the world consistently and unconsciously cooperate to flow smoothly in one direction on any pavement while an equally orderly flow exists for the other direction is a downright miracle. These flows ebb and change, but the integrity of the flows is incredibly robust when a large number of free willed people are on the move. There are no signs that people read and obey, there are no laws, nor are people programmed to move in these patterns. Regardless of the culture or area in the world, once a certain density of people is reached, the flows magically appear.

I say magically because how would anyone in the world today successfully exert this level of control over people all over the world in any matter? If we could understand how this works then perhaps we could find ways to dissolve a number of seemingly impossible societal problems.

When studying the behavior of many people, density is crucial. If you take those same people and put them in a huge pathless field, our freedom loving people will mill about completely at random just as common sense would suggest. But increase the density by either increasing the amount of people or decreasing the area they can walk on and at some critical point, smooth walking patterns suddenly emerge from no obvious rules or internal programming.

This is emergent behavior acting on people. These same orderly principles can be observed up and down all of reality. Don't let your familiarity with it mask the significance of its presence. For these same forces channel ants, not only into orderly lines, but into their entire social system. If you study some ant nests over time, you will notice that there is a birth, a youth (where it is vigorous and intent on action for the purposes of bettering its situation), a middle age (where it is more interested in maintaining successful patterns than initiating higher risk expansions), and eventually death of the nest. All through this process, the individual ants will live and die, but the system they make up will continue its orderly path. These forces also order flocks of birds, your brain, atoms and molecules, the weather, and so on and so on.

It is fascinating to watch nature's extraordinary, complex, and frequently beautiful patterns emerge from nowhere. These same forces act just as powerfully on us, right now, even as you read this. Luckily for us, these forces follow certain rules.

For example, on a crowded street, there are always some people that move against the flows. They are the exceptions to the rule. Before chaos theory became known, exceptions to the orderly flow of any system, be it electrons, bacteria, birds or people, were called "noise". Noise is always present in an emergent system. In fact, whenever I say "everyone…" I always mean "everyone, except those that constitute the noise in the system".

The people representing noise on a crowded pavement are the ones suddenly veering off the emergent pattern. They cut through the flows trying to get to a shop or onto another track, or they simply stop to talk. They are the ones that cause inefficiencies in the established flows. There are theoretical gains in efficiency to be made if we were able to rid ourselves of all the noise, but we would lose something crucial.

It is the presence of noise that allows the overall system to be able to respond to changes. Systems are always absorbing forces that are trying to change their shape. If a system is rigid, sometimes even small forces are beyond its ability to contain and the whole thing will collapse. Noise contains the necessary flexibility.

For example, if the best road starts to become busy, some drivers head for secondary roads in anticipation of gridlock. This is not as efficient but some people just don't like risking the possibility being caught in a traffic jam. As the volume of cars increase, even more drivers begin to make the wandering choice. These wandering drivers constitute noise in the system. They clog up the back roads while ignoring the best road for their journey. There are no objective gains for the individual or the system.

However, if still more cars enter the road system there will be a point where the optimal road suddenly becomes an optimal parking lot. Now the optimal route has changed. Suddenly, one (or several) of these wandering routes that previously constituted noise becomes the new best route. The change in numbers has changed the system.

A system becoming increasingly noisy is one of the first signs that something is forcing a change either internally or externally. While the established flows can sometimes absorb the pressure, occasionally the whole system has to shift. When this happens, the system looks to its noise, because that is where all the system's possibilities reside. If someone has found a better way to navigate a situation, others will soon follow. If the new way is sound enough to handle the increasing numbers of people, it will become the new optimal flow. Then the people hanging on to the old flow will become the "noise" that creates inefficiencies. And so it goes.

However, until the point of change is reached, all noise does is create inefficiencies in the system. There are no other benefits. That is why any system has a limited tolerance to the presence of noise.

Right now, all charity organizations that I am aware of are simply noise in the emergent flow of society. That is why they struggle and struggle to obtain little successes but rarely create the real change they crave. Even when it seems they have finally made a real difference to something important, the euphoria diminishes when the old patterns reassert themselves.

Because charities are noise, society can only tolerate their presence to a certain degree. Have you noticed that charities never grow beyond a certain point, even though businesses can go from garage to international power in only a decade or two?

Today, emergent flows can be modeled on computers using thousands or millions of little computer people (peoploids, some call them). This is very important for large events, because if large crowds are not handled properly people can be killed and injured from varies problems, like uncontrolled surges or the inability for an ambulance to reach a certain area. What the authorities do now is create an upcoming event on a computer to reveal what patterns emerge. Then they experiment until they find the best places for barriers and exits to maintain a healthy flow throughout the event. They can also simulate emergencies, like fire, to see how the crowd manages. This way the authorities can fine tune escape avenues, barriers and all the other things that are impossible to foresee using normal logic. In these situations, there are so many different possible interactions to consider that the number of potential combinations can move towards infinity (apologies to mathematicians). Luckily, we know that the overall emergent system will mask this internal complexity with a very stable and predictable exterior.

Creating the event on the computer allows an emergent system to solve all the problems simultaneously and present the likely flows. As such, most of these events run smoothly. Where the authorities use this modeling, people are rarely killed in rushing crowds as they were in the past.

Previously, the only other way to do this was to experiment every year (for a yearly event) trying to explore what works and what doesn't. But human common sense has little place in emergent pattern. Even experimentation has limited use. Events frequently evolved faster than the authorities could establish the best means of handling the old patterns.

Even though the details of governing crowded events are much more complex than the factors governing the flow of people on a crowed pavement, the overall characteristics remain the same. Once behavior emerges from the people, it will create a predictable pattern to anyone looking at it as a whole.

This is one of the paradoxes of emergent behavior. Even though a pattern for the whole exists, individuals can do whatever they wish at any time. Free will reigns and it does not change the overall pattern one iota. If fact, the freer people are in the system, the more robust and predictable will be the resulting emergent behavior.

Now isn't that a strange and wonderful thing?

How this affects us in the world as a whole is an important area to explore. Humankind is creating powerful and resilient patterns even though they may be invisible to many of us. Understanding how to re-shape these patterns becomes increasingly important as our power on earth increases. With this ability we can overcome a significant weakness in emergent behavior that is causing enormous problems for all of us.

The Great Flaw

Even before science defined emergent behavior, people instinctively recognized its existence. In 1776, Adam Smith wrote about an "invisible hand" that would guide the selfish desires of all people to do good for the society as a whole (in economic terms). Things were already moving towards what is known as a free trade economy, but Adam Smith understood what was happening. He realized that in order to allow the process of emergent behavior (the invisible hand) to create wealth for us all, we needed to let go of our attempts to control or better it. From the economy's point-of-view, these attempts would constituted noise that required energy to suppress. What Adam Smith instinctively realized was this energy could be released to create wealth instead.

The economy already had an overall guide of maximizing wealth in any given situation, and so reducing regulation unfettered the potential of the emergent system.

Many people at the time didn't understand it. The economist, Robert Heilbroner, has written about how difficult it might be to explain a free market system to a chief of a remote tribe. The tribal leader is traditionally responsible for the well-being of his people. His experience and knowledge guide when to hunt, and tradition and leadership then fairly distribute the food. All the people in the tribe trust in tradition and their leader for their success.

Try to imagine how you might explain how our economy is self-regulating, in spite of everyone having the freedom to do whatever they want, to someone who knows nothing of this. Before the free economic system came into being, we all used a mixture of tradition and command authority to guide our behavior. Imagine how hard it is to describe how a market economy works to someone who has never lived in one.

How would you explain it to a Chief of a tradition-bound tribe? The conversation might go something like this:

Chief: "If we need spears, who tells the men to make spears?"

Us: "No one. The men do what they want."

Chief: "But they are lazy. They will sit around and no one will have spears."

Us: "No, because they will realize that they need spears to eat."

Chief: "They won't care! They all want someone else to do it. Then no one will do it. We will all starve because we have no spears. People need me to tell them what to do, or we all starve."

Us: "Spears will be needed badly. Someone will make them because they can trade a lot for one. It will make them rich to make spears."

Chief: "So we must begin to starve before someone will make spear?"

Us: "Yes! I mean no! They will do it before then because they can trade for food."

Chief: "Why trade spear for food when anyone can hunt for their own food?"

Us: "Because some are better at spear making than hunting. Some are better at hunting than spear making. If everyone does only what they are best at, all your people will be better off."

Chief: "You don't listen. All my people know we need spears to hunt. Still, men lie around whether they are good at making spears or not. They do nothing until I tell them to make spears. If I don't say, they don't move. But I do say, they do move, and we all eat. It works. Why should we do this new mad thing you describe?"

Us: "You can organize only so much by yourself. This new system will organize everything for you and you can have unlimited growth."

Chief: "What system? Everyone just does what they want. That is no system."

Us: "People will want to do what is good for the tribe."

Chief: "You are mad man. Men are all lazy. No one will do anything and we will all starve. You are trying to kill us all." With that, she walks away.

It certainly does look mad, but can anyone doubt that the free market system works? The distribution might not be what people think is fair, but the free market economy has led to the creation of a staggering amount of economic wealth.

When the economy is freely allowed to evolve it will create incredibly rich and diversified solutions, just as Hillis' number sorting program did. The solutions are far more sophisticated than any individual or committee could possibly conceive.

The brilliance of Adam Smith was that he recognized how emergent behavior would deliver exactly what we needed without anyone having to tell people what to do. He also noticed that any time we interfered with the system by introducing laws or tariffs, or anything that hindered the freedom of the economy, it would reduce its ability to create wealth. He also noted, though he is not celebrated for this, that the system would be inherently unfair to many people and damaging to social systems.

But at the time, material wealth was very scarce, so its lure was much stronger than it is today. The fact that something could not only take over from direct human management, but also vastly improve on anything man had so far been able to command into presence, seemed like madness to many people at the time. It is amazing the resistance people have to the possibility that something could operate outside the human ability to conceive. But here we have an economy of such complexity that even the best minds that make economics their life's work are unable to successfully predict something quite simple, like how much the economy will grow in one year.

This complexity is the reason why the Soviet Union's economy collapsed. It tried to use a few brilliant people to command a more efficient and fair economy into existence. The ability to command an economy to a greater level of efficiency than an emergent system does not exist. The emergent system can simultaneously solve an uncountable number of problems with maximum efficiency. A human mind could not even hold in awareness all the elements that an evolving system routinely absorbs on a moment by moment basis.

However, the system is only as good as its inputs.

Economists have long since recognized that the economy is blind to entire areas, such as the environment. They call these externalities. Because of this, everyone has always thought it a good idea if we should allow the economy to take care of what it does see, while government legislation would take care of whatever the economy doesn't see.

But there is a problem with this model. Any legislation, popular action, charity concerts or anything not adhering to free-market principles will be seen as noise to be suppressed. Every human being on earth participating in the economy in any way is powering this suppression through our necessary but unconscious participation in human emergent behavior. If we try to directly confront of our own emergent system with legislation, we will fail. Just as the action of the number sorters was irrelevant to the overall drive towards becoming good number sorters, any action taken within our own emergent is just as ineffective. However, if we became aware enough to reach outside and reprogram our own emergent system, we could work miracles.

Right now, the economy is completely unaware that it is destroying the natural environment that currently feeds it. Like a drug addict, its vision is so narrow that it is content to maintain its position on its local peak, never noticing that the peak is rapidly descending. Even if the free will agents that make up the economic system (us) recognize this doom, it is largely irrelevant. Just as the economic planners of the Soviet Union were unable to better the emergent system of the economy, we cannot intellectually solve these entrenched problems.

The fact that the economy's voracious appetite for fossil fuels is creating a startling concentration of greenhouse gas in our atmosphere remains completely undetected by the economic system itself. As individuals we may stand horrified at a wall of destruction approaching us. It is like we are all driving towards a cliff at 80 mph while the system only allows a political debate on whether we can find a way to agree to reduce our speed by 20 mph or not. Some leaders fear that if they slow down they will be overtaken by others so they actually try to speed up. This is an unbelievably silly situation, but it is us that unconsciously powering it.

The remarkable circumstance in which we find ourselves has not arisen because politicians are stupid (with some possible exceptions) or evil (same caveat), but because they rose up through some of the most powerful emergent behavior filters we have. The whole political system is designed to make sure that only those who fully support the incumbent system succeed in gaining power. In a democracy, leaders must express the emergent behavior of the people (which has nothing to do with individual desires of the people) to remain in power.

All democratic leaders are expressions of the emergent behavior of their respective countries. They will not remain in power if they try to significantly deviate from the path dictated to them. What do you think would happen to any United States president if he suddenly decided that the Pentagon should be closed and the entire budget should be diverted into converting Americans to Buddhism? If we live in a true free willed society where people can do what they want, then why do you know instinctively that this is practically impossible? If the President really has a mandate to lead, then why can't it happen? If he doesn't have a full and complete mandate to do whatever he pleases, to what does he defer?

If America or any large democratic country goes to war, regardless of what you think, the emergent force within those countries permit it. In certain circumstances, it demands it. Have you noticed that whenever a governing party in a democratic country remains in power long enough it eventually ends up looking almost exactly like every other party that has had a lengthy time in power? It does not matter whether they began left wing, right wing, center or religious. Just as the little counting programs that were randomly created all ended up as number sorters, the political parties are being molded by the emergent system of society. This happens regardless of the desires of the leader or the party because, quite frankly, they are not the ones in control.

Every day we pollute. But this is not because we are stupid or ignorant; it is emergent behavior that is subtly, but very powerfully, moving us to a position that makes it impossible to avoid polluting. What do you think would happen to a government that really stepped up to the plate to shut down polluting activities? Let's say the British government priced petrol and heating oil at £100/litre. How long would they remain in power? Who, then, is in control? Global warming is only one of the possible consequences of continuing to allow humanity to remain unconscious. The same force prevents us from making real changes to help Africa and other poor areas; it prevents us from effectively tackling crime; and pretty much all other persistent social problems that appear to be "inevitable".

The same hidden force constraining government actions is also moving individuals. Right now, some people want everyone to individually decide not to pollute. We all recognize the problem, they say, and if everyone did something about it the problem would vanish. Technically this is true, but if we could solve society's problems by everyone recognizing the problem and then doing something about it, we would have been in Utopia thousands of years ago. This is no more feasible than the people of China and India deciding to stop developing in order to keep emissions down. Again, if the individual is not in power, then who is?

No matter where you stand there are no villains. If you think mankind is the villain, I'm afraid you will find every living creature on earth is subject to the forces of emergent behavior.

In the past, we have always blamed "others" when something hasn't gone as planned, but the fact is that most attempts to solve big societal problems have only been noise against the emergent forces of society. As long as they continue to try to change individuals (people or countries) instead of the emergent system, we will continue to be mysteriously drawn to repeat the old patterns, just as we are today.

We cannot succeed in commanding a cleaner economy into existence any more than the Soviets succeeded in commanding a fair economy into existence. Everything might look fine in the beginning, but the incredible complexity present in a true emergent system will soon reveal the flaws in any manufactured pattern. First little problems will appear, here and there, but then one will grow into a crisis. You may solve the first one, or even the first hundred, but eventually your manufactured system will reach a point where the pressure is too great and it will collapse into a proper emergent system with the proper amount of noise. The pattern will once again perfectly, but unconsciously, express the sum of all the forces present, visible and invisible.

The only way to tackle this in a sound and robust way is to engage the levers that directly influence the world emergent system. Otherwise, our emergent patterns will continue to blindly maximize for wealth and technology and we will be forced to participate in the collision into a wall of pollution and environmental degradation that has been foreseen for hundreds of years. So far, the proposed carbon quota system is the only solution I have heard that could engage the power of the economic emergent system. It is a limited solution, however, as it only tackles the problem of emissions from large factories and power plants. However, it must be implemented globally or it will not work. Also, the principles of emergent behavior must be properly understood or the implementation might end up looking like noise to the economy.

Just before this went to print, it was reported that European governments couldn't resist handing out so many carbon emission permits that carbon quotas effectively ceased to exist. This is just one example of how emergent systems suppress noise. This exactly the sort of thing will end if we can become aware and guide our own emergent behavior.

If we miraculously avoid the bullet of global warming, unconscious emergent patterns will inevitably lead us to another peril, not because it is inherently evil, but because it is programmed to create wealth and technology, not life. If we don't find a way to link our individual awareness to our own "mob consciousness", we are likely to be dragged kicking and screaming to a very unsavory doom.

By taking the effort to understand these forces, we have a chance of not only solving many terrible problems in the world, but also creating a real possibility of attaining an entirely different level of existence.

Harnessing the Power of Emergence

It might seem mad to some people that we are allowing our economic success to destroy the life-giving processes that got us here in the first place, but the fact is all emergent systems work this way, including nature. Mankind is no better or worse.

Evilness is simply not a factor here any more than the cormorants are evil for killing thousands of trees in Canada because their excrement is poisonous. They did not design their excrement, nor are they the first birds to find themselves with the desire to perch in trees. They are simply expressing how nature created them.

As of this writing, the efforts towards conserving elephants in a certain area of Africa have been a resounding success. But now there are so many elephants that they are literally destroying all the vegetation in their own habitat. Some people feel we have to intervene with a cull. Other people feel we should allow nature to take its course. The problem is that the elephant cycle is approximately 200 years long. In the intermediate times they decimate all the vegetation until there is almost nothing left. Most other medium and large animals die or leave because the elephants have destroyed their food supply. The elephants roam until their habitat is almost devoid of plants or animals. Then the inevitable happens. The elephants, after being completely dominant in their environment for generations, starve to death. This mass starvation finally reduces the pressure on the besieged vegetation allowing it to recover. Other animals can finally move back. The whole area teams with life. But then the elephant population starts to increase again…

Natural systems has no more foresight than our economy. It is a matter of luck as to which peak is climbed. Sometimes things magically balance out, but other times things go badly wrong.

As a group, humankind has exhibited no more awareness than any other living group. If we take out a lot of other species in our blind search for success, then we are not any different than the gray squirrel in the UK wiping out the red squirrel and numerous song birds in its relentless drive to increase its territory. If we kill off our food supply on earth and then experience mass starvation, let me assure you, we are following in the same well-trodden paths that has been used by nature many times.

Our economy is not inherently evil. What it does is maximize for what it sees, just like all natural processes. The only reason it does not notice the environment around it is because it has no mechanism for it to do so. It is like a leper who can no longer feel the cuts and scrapes and so leaves them to fester. There is no pain, but that lack of pain is exactly what can cause the behavior leading to death. Connections leading to pain can be crucial to life.

Most individuals within society do not want to witness the rest of nature laid waste by our economy. Because of this, many people feel like the economy is something separate from them, doing things that they do not approve of. The problem is that while emergent behavior results from individual behavior, it does not take into account the feelings or actions of individuals.

The reason any species damages its own surroundings is always the same; somehow immediate behavior has become disconnected from the health of its surroundings. If our economy is to become sensitive to the environment then links need to be created that are recognized by its own emergent behavior.

When nature does find a balance, it is the result of natural links. All balanced living systems on this planet are demonstrably linked with each other in an almost magical dance. There are so many examples of this balance that I will simply name a few for anyone who wants to look them up. There are ants that farm aphids to milk their sap, fish peacefully queuing up in a neat line that contains both predators and prey as they wait their turn to be attended to by cleaning fish, plants encouraging certain bacteria to make a home in them so that the plants can benefit from the bacteria's unique abilities. It goes on and on. A whole book could be written on this subject alone.

In all these cases, emergent behavior has created a maximization that benefits multiple species. Because the system has encompassed multiple interests, the entire ecosystem benefits from this powerful problem-solving mechanism. This can create a jump in the quality of life of all those involved. When nature is "balanced" in this way, it can look magical because the same forces that created number sorting solutions beyond our understanding are in action here. Instead of wealth and technology, the driving force of this emergent system is the creation and maintenance of life.

When new disease bacteria first emerge they can be lethal, but they will quickly evolve to become more benign for the simple reason that if they kill off the host, they kill off their food supply (remember that well-trodden path?). It is in their interest to keep us alive. However, it is not an example of forethought.

To simplify what happens, let's say a new disease bacterium emerges and there are two very similar strains. One is lethal to its host while the other is not. At first, the lethal bacterium has no advantage or disadvantage to the non-lethal bacteria. They both reproduce in their host in equal numbers. To the bacteria, it is irrelevant whether they kill or not. But after some time, the food supply in places that were populated mostly by the lethal bacteria become exhausted. Now the lethal bacteria cannot reproduce effectively anymore. However, places populated by the less lethal version have a reoccurring food supply, so they keep reproducing. Soon, it becomes the dominant bacteria. The lethal version becomes relegated to being part of the noise in the system of non-lethal bacteria.

The battleground then moves to our immune systems. The give and take, the maximizing of the success of everything continues in the emergent system that is the entire ecosystem.

If we put models with these principles onto computers, we get very similar patterns of infection to that which occurs in the real world. It is for this reason I feel we can say that it does not matter whether the germs are created by God, spirits, or are simply biological entities, because these principles can predict their actual behavior in the world. If a principle leads us to accurate predictions, does it matter whose lens is right?

Our economy is motivated by wealth creation and it has no connection or feedback systems that are linked with the environment. Because of this, as a species or resource declines, it does not recognize this as a problem to its prime directive of maximizing wealth at any given moment. What it will do is make whatever adjustments are necessary to maximize its output in the presence of a declining species. If the species is wiped out, then so be it. The economy will simply find a maximum within that new reality.

It is the same with pollution. Our economy will maximize itself regardless of the how much pollution is created. It does not notice pollution anymore than many of us notice how polluting our habits really are.

As long as people don't have to directly experience the pollution they create, there is nothing to tell them whether they pollute or not. However, we do know that people don't like it if pollution directly affects them. That is why we don't all have rubbish dumps in our back yard. If a few people around the edge of the dump complain, they are simply noise.

In terms of emergent behavior patterns, the problem is that the economy has no direct link to pollution. All solutions, such as taxes, fines and penalties, and treaties and agreements are all seen as noise to the economy. As such, it uses its power to minimize the presence of the noise so efficiency can be maintained. The United States central administration have been verbalizing this emergent imperative because they are the strongest expression of the dominant emergent system in the world, not because they are evil.

Quite simply, unless any introduced methods produce more wealth for the economy, they will be pressured to die out. This does not mean there have been no local successes, but local successes are irrelevant if the whole charges towards creating a worldwide rubbish tip. In fact, local successes can actually cause problems because people use their "common sense" and think that what works on a small scale must work on a large scale. But the system characteristics on a small scale can be profoundly different from the same system operating on a large scale.

In other words, if it works locally, it can be a spectacular failure globally. Later on we will use history to graphically demonstrate this.

What we need to do is go deeper and engage the power of the emergent pattern directly instead of trying to fight it. It might even be possible to do this without triggering a defensive response from its current wealth creation imperative.

This is a simplified example of how to harness the power of emergent behavior for our individual and societal benefit. This description is designed to demonstrate the mechanics in a simple way, so the detail of a real solution has been stripped away. If you feel I have oversimplified then perhaps you could think of a way to make the solution more realistic.

The problem is that society is very damaging to the natural environment that supports us. For the purposes of simplification only, we will pretend every family has a house and a yard. One way to directly harness the power of emergent behavior of society to solve this problem would be to make it so that everyone had to deal with their own rubbish.

Imagine if we had to bury all our own refuse in our own yard. Can you see how aware we would suddenly become of whether something we purchase is toxic or not? Or how much packaging there is on something we just bought? As our children are playing, how much oil from oil changes would we want in our back yard? Do you think effective recycling centers might take on a different urgency? In fact, automobiles in general might become endangered because they are incredibly polluting. We just don't see most of it. Old tires, all the broken bits that have been replaced...the list goes on and on. Whatever is not recycled goes in your back yard. Does anyone doubt the economy would change if this were ever to occur?

Did you notice the magical part? There is no policy or law that says we can't pollute. There is no campaign, no awareness drive, no studies, no lobbying; there are no committees, no pressure groups, no treaties, no charities and no new taxes. What would we do with all this unused money?

By the way, I hold a private pilot's license and use a fast Kawasaki ZX9R for my primary private transportation. So when I talk about losing vehicles I am not speaking safely from an eco-friendly cave home with a donkey parked outside. I know the loss it would be for some people, including myself. However, what is frequently not understood is that something equally fascinating will inevitably spring up. This might be a controversial statement, but the automobile is not the ultimate expression of excitement or manliness. It is not even the best we can do. Better and more exciting possibilities exist but the automobile's overwhelming presence effectively buries any other possible reality. It is a local peak and a very low one at that. Remember, emergent patterns can generate things that we have no ability to anticipate, both good and bad.

The simple act of shifting where we put our rubbish would have a fundamental effect on the face of the economy as a whole by drastically shifting the emerging patterns of our economy. We would be unbelievably clean without losing an iota of productive power. In fact, we would gain because we could dismantle the huge network that is currently needed to keep our own rubbish away from us.

None of the excitement of our developing economy would be lost, but the new economy would take an unprecedented level of responsibility for the mess it makes. This would not be perfect, because there is always noise in any system, but the pollution levels will likely be well within nature's ability to handle on its own.

If you accept that this method might be a possibility, then you will be glad to know we can use the exact same method to solve all sorts of problems that we consider unsolvable today. For just about any problem that charities now struggle with as they try to bring change and healing to some ugly part of our society, there is a permanent solution. Even if I personally don't know the correct way to reconstruct the emergent patterns for all our problems, I know that a way exists. I would love to hear from others if you have ideas. I need to, because I am only an expert of my own lens. For the full picture, I need experts in as many other lenses as possible to engage in this.

Another paradox that we will examine later on is that even though the emergent pattern is immune to the free will of the individuals within, every single person has an enormous impact in the future development of our society. Every single one of your actions counts, just not in the way you thought it did.

It might take some effort before we recognize all the control levers in our society's emergent behavior, but the sooner we start the sooner we will regain control. Every step we take will move our society closer to becoming a responsible and self-determining inhabitant of the earth.

Those Who Have Come Before

I have to admit, that when I first conceived the idea of this work, the problem of proof was very worrisome. If I used anything other than real people there would always be those that claimed that since I wasn't using real people, these concepts have no validity. It is true that I haven't experimented on any societies, but it is also irrelevant, in the same way that I don't need to throw real people from a cliff to prove gravity works on people as well stones.

Fortunately for me, reality comes to the rescue, because there were societies that engaged emergent behavior in a way that took them to very high peaks of happiness. While staying connected with the nature around them, these cultures contained all the principles necessary to harness the power of emergent behavior in a constructive life-giving way. In some of the most successful societies crime was non-existent. They lived a rich and rewarding life while also nurturing the environment around them. Some of the most developed of these societies were those of the Native Americans before 1492.

It might surprise some that in spite of this sustainable and nurturing lifestyle, they were very adventurous and inquisitive. Before the Europeans found them, some American societies had considerably more advanced scientific and medical knowledge than the Europeans at the same time. For example, they discovered the concept of zero in their math long before it came to be in use in Europe. As this was very threatening to certain beliefs at the time, the evidence was largely destroyed and the information suppressed. Luckily, the attempt to wipe the evidence from existence was not totally successful or we would not know about it now.

Unfortunately, much of the detailed history that these societies had recorded was lost during these purges. As such, we cannot track the detail of how these societies developed and evolved over time. All we are left with are scraps of information and stories that survived the destruction and more recent archaeological discoveries with which to reconstruct their past experience.

Even the European archives are a little misleading. The disease that the Columbus expedition had introduced into the Americas had wiped out an enormous percentage of the population. The societies we all came to know were simply the remnants. None of the Europeans, except the very earliest European explorers, experienced the healthy Native American societies. For the cause of colonization and certain belief systems this was all good, because the evidence suggests that the Europeans would have been wiped off the continent if they had faced the full might of the Native American civilizations.

When Columbus first arrived, it is estimated that there were one hundred million people living in the Americas. They were acknowledged to be absolutely superb hunters. The capital city of the Aztecs had four times the number of people as London did at the same time. It was well within their capability to annihilate all the large animals in their area. But, like the great barrier reefs, these societies fostered an enormous respect for nature.

What is the evidence? In a land inhabited by millions of the best hunters in the world, the first Europeans were in awe of the sheer quantity of animals and fish that lived there. By reading some of the letters sent back to Europe during this time, you can experience their awe at the rivers filled with fish, forests filled with deer, the pristine beauty of the new land. Many things they disliked about Europe were absent.

The water and the land were free of pollution. It seemed like paradise to many of the Europeans, even though millions of people had lived there for centuries with advanced forms of government and science. In many cases there were no policemen or jails and the people were completely free to do as they pleased. Of course, since their emergent patterns created a tendency to avoid crime, letting people do what they wanted was not the political suicide it would be today.

Can you imagine the money we would save if we could realistically dismantle the justice system?

In nature, coral reefs are built by animals for their own selfish purposes, but because they are intricately linked with all life around them, the reefs themselves become a catalyst for even more life to flourish. If you want to swim with fantastic fish, in both quality and quantity, reefs are where you want to be. There are many structures in nature which, although ultimately built for one purpose, become beacons and nurturers for all sorts of life.

Because of this, the emergent patterns of all of nature will try to sustain these places. Nothing in nature wants to destroy a reef, because it harms no one and sustains so many. However, this is not true of man's structures. Just like the elephants in Africa, we harm many, and very few (some rodents, certain insects, and disease) gain. It is ironic that the reefs are being killed off as a result of our unconscious activity.

The Native American communities were surrounded by a full rich eco-culture just as the great barrier reefs are in the sea.

But this is a trivial accomplishment compared to another amazing feat. These Americans were largely disease free. According to their stories, they had very few pandemics, or epidemics, or very much at all that killed them.

It wasn't because the Americans had exceptionally strong immune systems. When the Europeans arrived, the diseases they carried nearly obliterated the Americans. In just one hundred years after Columbus landed, in the single lifetime of an elder, the Native American population had dropped from one hundred million to only ten million. Only one person in ten was left standing. There is no society in the world that would not be devastated by such a loss. They were an entire culture in grief. Not only that, they had lost most of their generals, elders, and healers—meaning that their knowledge and experience base had been almost obliterated. Their capacity as a society had taken a shocking blow. Since emergent patterns change with numbers, the original societal emergent patterns had long since been destroyed by the time the Europeans began a proper study of these cultures. Their conclusions were frequently in error as a result, including the underestimation of the Native American "medical system". Its tremendous effectiveness was not recognized for centuries.

So, if their relative disease free status had nothing to do with a strong immune system or an elaborate and expensive health system, how did it work?

Bacteria: Our Partner in Life

Bacteria are amazing creatures. They can do things that all other creatures find impossible. Their specialties are so useful that both plants and animals create homes inside their bodies for bacteria to live and do their magic. Human beings are one example. If you took all the bacteria out of your stomach, for example, you would hardly be able to digest anything. You would starve.

But the interest of any bacteria is successfully living and reproducing. They help us not because they are friendly, but because living inside us creates a stable environment for them to raise their children, so to speak. They break down food for us so we can absorb it, and they get a lifetime free catering service. Everyone is happy.

Other bacteria take a more direct approach. Instead of being a partner in our biology, they try to dodge our immune system. If successful, they can happily reproduce as well. But if their colonies get too big, we become ill.

If we model these principles on a computer it will replicate how bacteria behave in the real world. As such, it doesn't really matter if the principles are right or not because we can use them to successfully predict how the bacteria will evolve, and how to combat disease. Viruses follow similar rules, though I am not personally aware of any "friendly" viruses.

Germs, like all living systems, use the power of emergent behavior to survive. In Western societies, we are using our brains to try to stop them. We are trying to command health into existence in the face of a natural emergent system. Unfortunately, our "annihilate everything bad" approach threatens the survival of these emergent living systems. This is a declaration of war against one of the most powerful and successful living problem-solving forces on earth.

Just like Pearl Harbor was for the Japanese, at first, there can be some spectacular successes. The eradication of smallpox (coincidentally one of the main diseases that killed off the Native Americans) was a huge battle won. However, little weaknesses soon started to appear. The bacteria's emergent system found a solution to our antibiotics. Our marvelous technological achievement was suddenly rendered useless. No matter, we'll invent more and better antibiotics. Then it turned out that the emergent system of bacteria was much more effective at combating a threat to its existence than we are at commanding colds out of existence. Now, because of our attempt to detach ourselves from the natural system around us, our own natural immune system is beginning to get out of touch with what is going on out there. Several new diseases are popping up and turning out to be remarkably insubordinate to our commands for them to die.

As in any command system that is attempting to replace an emergent system, these weaknesses will grow until the system as a whole starts to shudder with instability. Believe it or not, we might even end up with a potential global pandemic on our hands.

All germs make up living systems. If you took out all the bacteria and viruses from our bodies, we would die. If you took all of mankind out of the ecosystem, the germs would barely notice. In the great game of life, who do you think sits in a more powerful position?

It is rarely wise to declare war on something on which your own life depends. It makes as much sense to declare war on oxygen. Of remote interest, the antioxidants that are so prevalent in the health news are nature's way of removing the harmful free ranging oxygen molecules from your cells. Too much oxygen can lead to death. It is the right balance of anything that is healthy.

So, what if we were to re-enter the natural world and learn to coexist with the bacteria and viruses that make up the ecosystem? How would that look?

The original Native American societies' belief systems contained a powerful understanding of how natural substances could restore the balance to sick people, a knowledge that is only now being confirmed after over 500 years of denial by science and religion. But we have yet to catch up to a fraction of the capabilities of the Native American healers in this respect.

The belief system of the Native Americans contained within it a remarkable understanding of how to use the power of emergent forces to continually raise their life experience while remaining fully attached to the natural world around them. They became experts in the use of emergent behavior as a problem-solving tool.

Just like the Jarawa, their belief system did not resemble anything the Europeans respected. The Native Americans were considered unsophisticated godless heathens. In an enormous effort by both church and state to bring God and modern knowledge to the Native Americans, they destroyed one of the most powerful life-giving social systems humankind has ever known.

Unfortunately, as things stood, it was inevitable. The unconscious power of the European emergent system was responsible for this. Even today, though it would look different, no one could have stopped it from happening. For those who might wonder how that might look today, perhaps observing what is happening in the Middle East right now might be a worthwhile investigation. There is a question as to whether those who are intent on remaking the Middle East in their image are aware of the treasures that reside in the Middle Eastern belief systems and culture. If not, then I would suggest that there might be a possibility for a great deal of unconscious damage to occur. Sometimes the impact of treasures lost can reverberate far beyond political boundaries.

The Native Americans' beliefs made them strive to find a balance with everything. As they explored the environment around them, they used their intelligence and inquisitiveness to determine how everything they found could create a higher order balance in their lives. Everyone had different interests, but the healers were fascinated by how the plants affected people in so many different ways. Soon, they knew which parts of nature helped re-establish the balance in the body. This method is important to bacteria and viruses because it did not attempt to wipe them out. The germs' survival as a system was not threatened. It is possible that the healers managed to establish constant stable relationship with colonies of bacteria and viruses that allowed the people to live a remarkably disease-free life. If this happened, then the traditional healers managed to establish self-sustaining balance that benefited everyone and everything in the long-run.

The way it worked it this; if a colony of germs embraced an overly ambitious growth rate the person would became ill. The medicine used would put pressure on the system as a whole to restore the balance between the germs and the person. What it would not do is attempt to eradicate them entirely. The colony would diminish (but not disappear) and the person would feel well again.

Like the flows that crowded people adhere to on pavements, this was a flow that was established between the Native Americans and their environment. We have no record of how they got there and because these long nurtured flows were completely destroyed by the time we were examining them. We do not actually know how successful they really were. We do know that the Native Americans thought the ways of the Europeans were very dangerous. They feared that the "white man's ways" would eventually threatened long-term survival of everyone on earth.

If you pressure the survival of any living system, it will fight back with all the power at its disposal. Just like Hillis' evolved number ordering solutions, a living system's emergent power can easily create solutions that are impossible for us to imagine before they occur and, sometimes, impossible for us to understand full stop. This could make winning a campaign of annihilation against disease rather difficult.

However, if we find the balance point for both systems, a state of cooperation will inevitably arise. This lesson is well illustrated by a sociology tool called the prisoner's dilemma.

What follows is only a brief explanation, but the principles and the rules are covered in much more detail in the chapter called The Rise and Fall of Tit For Tat.

This is something that can be done with any pair of people. Each person has to make a choice to either cooperate or deviate, without a clue as to what the other player is going to do. One way to do this is by labeling cards and then having each player place one card on the table simultaneously.

As each player can make one of two moves are only four possible outcomes for each turn and they are scored according to the table below.

		PLAYER A			
		Cooperate		Deviate	
PLAYER B	Cooperate	A: +3	B: +3	A: +5	B: -1
	Deviate	A: -1	B: +5	A: +1	B: +1

If your opponent cooperates, you score 5 if you deviate, but only 3 if you cooperate.

If your opponent deviates, you score 1 if you deviate, but you lose 1 if you cooperate.

No matter what your opponent does, the best score is always achieved by deviating. Obviously, the rational reaction is to deviate. Things look bad for the side of cooperation. At this level of awareness, most people would naturally climb the "survival of the fittest" peak.

Hold on, haven't we come to understand that what may be successful locally can lead to failure globally?

To expand our awareness we need to allow the players to have several turns to let the patterns emerge, because this deceptively simple model creates fascinating results. If we combine both players' score instead of allowing the individuals to remain disconnected, an entirely different picture emerges. As soon as some deviation appears, the highest possible combined score of the two players is (5 + (-1)) =4 per turn, whereas the cooperators' combined score will be (3+3) = 6 per turn.

A system producing 6 per turn will exist at a higher state than one producing only 4. Even though the best individual score is always obtained by deviating, over time cooperators working together will always earn more.

When we measure policies and actions against individual gain we can miss huge opportunities for ourselves as individuals in a connected society. In actual research many people naturally descended into round after round of deviating and therefore generated only a combined score of 2 per turn. This generates the lowest possible score for this system as a whole. Survival of the fittest may offer tremendous individual reward but it is the lowest possible existence for a system as a whole.

This is what the poor people of the world have been saying for centuries. But the solution is not to have the rich people give wealth to poor people. This is simply noise in the system. At the extreme, it would instantly impoverish the world, just as it did recently in Zimbabwe. The current economic system is designed to reward successful individuals with huge sums, but this pattern prevents society from reaching its full potential. This holds back everyone, including the richest and most powerful people in society today.

The Western model of medicine is another manifestation of survival of the fittest. Medicine might win one round, but disease is not going to give up when its very survival is at stake. Even if one particular disease is successfully annihilated there are thousands more waiting in the wings. Not only that, but the most successful germs will now be the ones that can maximize reproduction in the shortest period possible, before man has a chance to react. Therefore, the new strains have no reward for being benign. There is no longer any advantage of not killing the host. If you are a germ, the best thing is to completely overwhelm the immune system of a person and reproduce as quickly as possible before humankind reacts with its annihilation response. There is a likelihood that we are training the new strains to become as lethal as possible.

The Native American model was to join with these living systems in a cooperative dance. Since germs were not being exterminated it was the benign ones that were the most successful. If you kill a host that is not going to kill you, all that has been accomplished is the loss of a food source. Just like the prisoner's dilemma, the germs and the people settled down to round after round of cooperation. Both gained the largest reward.

For the Native Americans, it was horrifying to have the European's forcing them to give up the life sustaining flows they had nurtured for centuries in favor of such a harsh new reality. It seemed like they were being forced to sow the seeds of death by a blind but impossibly powerful people. There is a important lesson for them that is contained in this experience.

It took over five hundred years before science recognized that the medicines of the Native Americans were effective. Unfortunately, this knowledge is not being used to maximize life as the Native Americans did. Instead of being a part of a carefully crafted emergent flow, these newly rediscovered indigenous medicines are being refined to become killers. This refinement reduces what could have been a sustainable system to a single bullet to be fired in the war against disease.

Learning to Play

Chess has only a few simple rules. A person could easily learn them in a day. However, what chance do you think they would have in winning a world chess tournament that evening? The real challenge of any new game is learning how to use the rules effectively in a real environment.

Trying to foresee in our heads what kind of environment would be created by a certain set of rules is usually unsuccessful. There are simply too many factors to consider. Our head is not made for this kind of calculation. As such, without experience the game rules alone tell you very little about how to win chess at a world championship level.

There is an ancient East Asian strategy game, called Go in the West, that has far fewer rules to learn. Interestingly, it is much harder to master. The environment that emerges from Go's simplicity is extremely subtle and complex. It takes only a few minutes to learn all the rules but a lifetime to learn how to win.

Life is very similar except that is has pretty much an unlimited number of rules. Not only that, but the rules frequently change, especially in today's fast moving society. The principles of emergent behavior are one of the key measurable manifestations of the rules of life. However, it will not give up its treasures for someone who has simply learned the rules. It can take quite some time before the magic coalesces before our eyes.

We can see this in the behavior of teenagers, people who suddenly find themselves in near adult bodies with near adult brains. Their sudden new awareness unfilled by experience makes it seem like they know and understand far more than they actually do. They might be aware of the adult rules, but many can't understand the reasons behind them. To them, rules seem arbitrary, whose only real design is to keep them down. So they rebel. It will take them years before they have had enough life experience to understand why the accepted rules are important for everyone. But by then, they are no longer teenagers. They are the next generation of old codgers complaining about how teenagers have no respect.

Teenagers are not stupid. How can older people reasonably expect the current crop of teenagers to behave within constraints being promoted by people who refused to adhere to them when they were teenagers themselves?

Because of their lack of experience, teenagers also are poorly equipped to recognize the different peaks of society. They are launched into life through a combination of upbringing, environment and personality, but just about anyone I have questioned acknowledges that their teenage years were about reaction, not evaluation and awareness of their possibilities. As in Hillis' number sorting programs, this random collection of people all head for the peaks and will climb one of the first bases they come across with no real awareness of where they are headed. Some end up on low local peaks and some find the rare high ones, but almost none of them are aware of the consequences of their decisions until much later in life. This is why children and teenagers are so susceptible to addictions and other damaging behavior. It feels good now and there is little awareness of other peaks around them. The understandings necessary to successfully navigate a living system like society comes with life experience.

That fact is we become more and more aware of how the rules of life work the older we get. The people in the best position to possess wisdom about the flows of life are the aged. It would follow that a society that has found a way to work with their own emergent patterns would also have a place of great respect for their elderly.

But for this wisdom to grow, it has to be planted as early as possible. I would like to list some of the "rules" and characteristics of emergent behavior.

1) One must have a population. It doesn't matter if they are ants, people, electrons, or programs. It doesn't matter if they are aware or not.

2) They have to be able to communicate with others in their group in some form, even if that just means bumping into each other.

3) Emergent systems only exist as a flow. There is no information about the emergent system in an instant. Cutting a part of it out and looking at it under a microscope will reveal much about that part and practically nothing about the system.

4) The characteristics that emerge are determined by rules that themselves emerge. These characteristics are completely unrelated to the characteristics of a participating individual. A common mistake is to think emergent behavior is the

same as aggregate behavior (the sum of everyone's behavior). Emergent behavior is causal to aggregate behavior, but not the other way around.

5) Changing the number of individuals will, at critical points, change the emergent characteristics, sometimes radically.

6) Emergent systems are a perfect expression of the state of an open-ended number of constantly changing facts, variables and laws.

There are uncountable different emergent systems at many different levels in reality. Some might be quite destructive while others are beneficial. The influence of each system waxes and wanes like waves on the sea, but there is usually one that dominates a particular environment. In human society, that emergent system is currently the free market economy. Its connections are designed to create wealth but it is not in any way connected to human happiness. As such, it frequently does not empower our best interests.

As we become more familiar with emergent systems we will be able to transform them to suit our needs and that of the world. But we will have to put some effort into understanding them.

For some, the best way to become familiar with something is to see it working in the real world. The next few chapters are for these people.

The War on Iraq

Countries, like all evolving systems, have phases. Frequently, the young phase is all to do with action. As countries grow into later phases, action is replaced by a tendency towards influence, talk and negotiation. Like all ageing systems, they become more aware of the impact and influence of action within complex systems. Through experience, they have learned that patterns are far more resistant to change than the young hope. All that dashing action that looked so promising in the beginning rarely brings about permanent or intended changes. In some cases, hopelessness sets in. This can lead to too little action. This is the stage where moaning without action occurs. This drives the young crazy. If someone doesn't like something, then why don't they do something about it? And on it goes.

Now, it would be easy to look at the United States and say that it got too excited about commanding the world to be fixed through direct intervention. It is possible to look at the United Kingdom and suggest it was forsaking its accumulated wisdom in order to reclaim its youthful vigor and glory by joining a "gang" that was about to express its dominance through the immense destructive power of war. In fact, both these countries were acting out in accordance to what we empowered them to do. Because the mechanism is not understood, many people still seek to separate themselves from these actions.

When a problem occurs, society initiates the search and shame mission to find a person or organization that is the Villain. Have you noticed how the media has been stoking the fires of dissatisfaction? But the media isn't the Villain here either. As it says to us, it has to report what interests its audience. The media definitely influences what we want to think, but we not only allow it, we demand it.

Within an emergent system, the pressure to do as it dictates is subtly irresistible. The United States keeps insisting that it is the leader of the free world. The rest of the world wonders when the election was that they obviously missed. However, whenever military or economic leadership is required, the world has so far looked to the United States for leadership.

Just as the emergent system of countries have powerful mechanisms in place to make sure its leaders only act to support it, the character of the United States is being influenced by the world-wide emergent system to champion its principles of wealth creation and technological growth. In other words, the system made up by everyone in the world has helped to shape the international character of the United States. Is it any wonder that the United States champions technology and democratic free markets as the ultimate solution? The people who feel ethically superior to the United States are frequently those who are the least conscious of these connections.

The war on Iraq was one expression of a world-wide emergent system. If you participate in the economy then you were part of the world-wide emergent force that attacked Iraq, even if you were an Iraqi Sunni soldier. Just as it was useless for Hillis' little programs to protest against becoming better number sorters, it was useless for us to protest against war that the world-wide emergent system had decided must happen.

These forces have been articulated by the British Prime Minister trying to justify his decision to go to war. He keeps insisting that anyone in his position would have made the same decision. He is absolutely right. The emergent system of the United Kingdom filters the population searching for people whose thoughts and actions would best support the system and then put him or her into power. The closer one is to thinking like a "leader", the more the system empowers them to become leaders. Those people with radical views constitute the noise in the system and are subtly but powerfully guided away from true power positions.

While some might think this is "evil", without these controls, our society would be very chaotic. If we were swinging from socialists to right wing to green to martial with each election, there would be great uncertainty throughout society. Complexity requires a stable environment in order to form, and many social structures enhancing our lives would be missing. All successful cultures and societies need the stabilizing force of emergent systems, but unless we take the time to become aware of the nature of our own emergent systems, especially as we pass through critical numbers, we open ourselves to some very unpleasant possibilities.

Remember the villain who rose up in Germany in the 1930s? Hitler was an expression of the system that arose from the ashes of 1918. No single man can force millions of people to do his will. He needs those millions of people to help him. How did Hitler suddenly find an entire country willing to aid him in some very dubious operations? Most Germans knew what was going on in Germany, but they couldn't reconcile the disconnection between how Germany's emergent system was guiding them to act and their personal beliefs about right and wrong. So they chose to see nothing.

What is the difference between this and what is going on with global warming today? Allowing emergent behavior to arise without consciousness is a very dangerous game to play.

The Middle East is feeling persecuted because it is. It describes its attackers as the "West", but this is simply their sense of the economic emergent system trying to suppress noise in the system. This is why some Muslims talk about world-wide revolutions. They instinctively know that the true cause of the forces trying to change them come from a much broader base than just a few countries. What they don't understand is that they are also part of the "western" system that they say is evil.

The suicide bombers are just as involved as a New York businessman. However, the suicide bomber is part of another emergent system that has formed in response to what is happening in the Middle East. The war on terrorism is like the war on disease and will be just as effective and just as costly.

By the way, if the Muslims did manage to initiate a revolution and institute Sharia Law over all the world, the result would be very similar to that described in the next chapter.

Before the West marched in to dismantle Saddam Hussein's regime, there were several functioning emergent systems nurturing the Iraqi people. Both the economy and society depends on the effectiveness of these systems in order to function properly. Instead of protecting the integrity of these systems, the West rolled in with a conscious intent to cripple the infrastructure. It worked. They killed off many of the emergent systems that supported the civilians of Iraq. Those controlling this attack then activated their plan to command these structures to return.

Economies and societies contain many layers of emergent systems which support the people within. It can take years for these systems to build themselves into life-sustaining entities. Many developing communities and countries will be happy to tell you just how unbelievably difficult it is to get an economy to transform itself from a weak shadow of possibility to one that creates usable wealth for its people. Western developers seem to forget that the West's miracle of wealth creation took hundreds of years of nurturing to develop. Just as you would expect, not even the presence of enormous wealth will enable a healthy or wealthy system to emerge. Iraqis used to enjoy a quality of life equal to the West, but the war has reduced the country to third world conditions, in spite of the presence of enormous wealth in the form of oil.

What chance do you think Africa has?

Just as the Soviets didn't recognize the presence of emergent systems in successful economies, the thinkers behind the Iraq strategy did not recognize how little control they actually had in recreating the life-giving systems they had just destroyed. It looked to me like they thought they could command a society, an economy, and a democracy simultaneously into existence. All these things may be simple conceptually, but they are unbelievably complex systems that need great wisdom to effectively nurture into reality. Just as with the number sorting program, many of the solutions exist outside normal human awareness, no matter how much some of the leaders involved claim they understand (or are "inspired").

As with all emergent systems, none of these systems can be controlled directly, especially by people who do not acknowledge their existence. An enormous sum of money and planning went into an attempt to command a functioning society into existence. It failed. People in charge of projects were moved around. Massive amounts of resources, including the US expenditure of over $20,000,000,000 of Iraq's own savings, vanished into a black hole of ineffectiveness. (This has led to a US criminal investigation)

People were killed and continue to be killed through random violence as of this writing. In the years that the West has had control inside Iraq, the basic standard of living and security that Saddam Hussein's citizens previously enjoyed has still not been recovered. People lost the expectation of reliable running, electricity, and a predictable existence on the streets. There is a reasonable chance that the overthrown regime will eventually be replaced by one that is even more radical.

Using an army and army discipline to rebuild a society is a very bad idea. The military is internally structured to factor out emergent forces as much as possible. Whatever cannot be controlled will be killed, and emergent forces cannot be controlled, at least not directly. For a soldier, this is life and death. As such, the military has the least amount of expertise in these living systems of any of our organizations.

Their natural desire will be to try to command everything they touch. They want to squash all inefficiencies out of the system. Noise must be eliminated. If you are in war for your survival, this is a good thing, but if you are trying to nurture a growing society and economy, this will lead to disaster. Just like the Soviets' economy, just like the coalition in Iraq, and just like New Orleans after hurricane Katrina, trying to replace any emergent system with a command structure will fail. We do not have even a fraction of the awareness required to enable us to solve problems in complex systems (like a culture or society) that emergent systems routinely solve without effort.

If we suddenly had to consciously take over all our automatic body functions we would die. Our brains are not equipped to deal with so many factors simultaneously to keep us alive. We have enough trouble trying to decide if one single food causes cancer or not. Imagine us trying to constantly make those decisions at a life and death level every moment of our entire life. Not only couldn't we do it, but why would anyone want to?

Emergent forces have the potential to lift our situation beyond our ability to understand. Trying to replace these forces with our intelligence is a waste of time because no matter how intelligent anyone is, it is the wrong type of intelligence. If we are to raise the state of our existence we must learn to use emergent behavior to effectively allow our potential to unfold. What we have been doing is no longer adequate. Without a working awareness of emergent behavior, things will continue to go badly wrong, regardless of what people think they know.

With a working knowledge of our own emergent behavior, we have a real possibility of entering into an entirely different age in human history.

When Emergence Pounces

No matter what the intent is of the people involved, once a critical mass has been reached, emergent forces will take over. If these forces remain disconnected from our awareness, as they have been throughout history, then we do not control our own destiny. There is no command authority that can override emergent behavior once it has been activated.

The emergent system of science had a part in destroying the knowledge of the Native American societies because it did not recognize that form of that wisdom. Today, it is unconsciously active in suppressing the validity of all the other belief systems other than itself, especially faiths and spirituality. We have yet to count the cost of this action but it is certainly contributing to the radical groups we have springing up all over the world.

Sometimes what emerges is good and sometimes it is not. Without the effort to bring this into awareness, we are allowing ourselves to be blown about by a wind that is completely unaware of our needs, desires, or any greater good. Even the best organizations can have their intentions twisted without it being anybody's fault. It is not a sign of incompetence or the presence of evil. It is simply the way behavior emerges in large groups.

The Christian church is a fascinating study because its entire history has occurred in relatively recent times and is well documented. Within the Christian faith, as with other faiths, there lies great wisdom. This is the story of how emergent behavior destroyed the potential expression of that wisdom.

Just after the time marked by the birth of Christ, Christians appeared in small groups. They were a gentle people given to living their non-violent belief by example. They were frequently martyred in their attempt to bring a new gentle way to the violent world around them. They continued to spread the belief that if we acted on the few good rules found in the Bible and the teachings of Christ then we could find ourselves in a peaceful nurturing world. Given what was going on at the time, it was a hugely attractive vision.

The dominant power in Europe during this time was the Romans and, according to the people who study this culture, the Romans saw cruelty as an admirable trait in their leaders. Having a group selflessly stand up in the face of such cruel power and saying that leaders should be nice to their servants and that everyone being nice to each other would create a better world, was quite radical indeed. At first, they were dismissed as a fringe religion, but the Christians had an ace up their sleeve.

Christians believed that the poor could be as holy as the rich and powerful. It was another radical idea at the time. Not surprisingly, it was an extremely attractive proposition to the many servants and slaves. Suddenly, one's station in life was no longer an indication of the magnificence of one's soul.

Of course, none of this seemed like a good idea to those who believed that wealth and power were the earthly indication of the favor of the Gods, especially if they had gone to great lengths to prove that worth. This conflict grew worse as some servants and slaves began to feel that men who pursued wealth and power had less chance of entering the kingdom of God than a camel has of passing through the eye of a needle. This attitude was not missed by their masters. The old established belief system began to feel threatened and swung into action.

The Christians endured massacres and torture. But they clung to their belief of the goodness of a gentle society, feeling in their hearts that God and their faith would prevail and all this abuse would stop for everyone throughout the world.

The Christian movement survived this trial by fire until Constantine took the entire Roman Empire into Christianity. Shortly after, the Roman Empire collapsed.

This left a huge vacuum of power. People could believe pretty much anything they wanted. Is it surprising that the poor and powerless mass of humanity chose the religion that promised that the meek would inherit the earth? The numbers of Christians swelled.

As we have seen, once the numbers pass a certain point, emergent behavior can radically redefine the characteristics of any organization. This occurs in many new organizations. In the beginning, when their numbers were small everything worked just as planned. Then they passed the critical point. Just like on the pavement, the forces of emergent behavior quietly and invisibly exerted themselves on the group.

Many founders of new movements are heartbroken when this suddenly occurs in their ranks. They wonder what went wrong. Everything was so good when it was small. Now, all these new people are ruining everything!

At the core of Christianity lies the bible, the holiest document of the Christian faith. Within these pages it is written that its followers shall not kill. This is a direct commandment from God. There is no greater authority in the whole universe for a Christian. This was reinforced when Christ said that people must love their neighbor.

These facts alone should have ensured an increasingly gentle and peaceful world as the power of the Christians ascended throughout the world. It would make sense to believe that if you were a faithful Christian who had the one true loving God clutched in your heart, read the bible regularly and lived its teachings as best you could, you would be safe in a Christian-dominated society.

As history demonstrated, this was not the case. God's commandment and Jesus' words were not enough to stop the Protestants and the Catholics from murdering and torturing each other on a grand scale.

If this was the case for good Christians, what chance do you think the bad Christians had? This question is answered by an exhibition of the very best that age had to offer in the art of intimidation, torture, and murder; the Holy Inquisition. How about non-Christians? Well, the Holy Crusades burned their way into any culture that tried to resist the expansion of the Christian faith. Heathens had a choice of conversion or destruction.

As with all systems large enough to generate an emergent system, commandments will not work, even if the authority is God. Emergent behavior eventually created officially sanctioned arguments to allow Christians to break the commandments. What this meant was that where the scriptures supported the emergent system they were enforced as holy. But where they didn't, a superior understanding was manufactured. Thou shall not kill became a convenience depending on the situation relative to the larger church. The Bible became subservient to the imperatives of emergent behavior.

Some Christians far from the center might quite readily recognize the patterns I am describing, but the people near the center will have much more difficulty. The emergent patterns will always create very compelling arguments. They are logically sound and the information at hand will appear as unassailable proof for their position. For many of these people, it will take an exceptional act of will or awareness to perceive the reality outside that dictated by emergent behavior.

Today, in small groups, Christian communities can be among the most nurturing in society. Their principles of connection to each other have the potential to create a deep human contentment that is difficult to demonstrate to those on the outside. In these communities, the numbers are too small for emergent behavior to prevent the wisdom of the belief from expressing itself.

In order for any belief to grow beyond the lifetime of its originators it has to possess a method to survive and grow in the presence of many other competing beliefs and forces. Just as a person must have an immune system to live in the presence of germs, any mature belief system will have an array of weapons at its disposal to see off any threat. If its weapons are not strong enough, it will disappear.

The Christian church has survived many centuries, so it was indeed successful in ensuring its survival. At its peak, the church commanded armies that could, and frequently did, threatened countries. It had tremendous sway over the day-to-day affairs of all European governments. Just like the authorities to whom they had previously martyred themselves in the beginning of their own history, the Church used its influence and power to wage wars, influence governments and amass huge fortunes.

It is crucially important to understand that this was not the fault of the Christians or their belief. It was a direct result of the same emergent forces that are present within any large, successful organization. The same thing happened to Gandhi's movement when it grew beyond a certain size. When violence first appeared in his movement, Gandhi was so distressed he almost died. This fact temporarily suppressed the violence, but Gandhi's final fate was to be assassinated and only a few decades later India joined the ranks of nuclear powers in the world. Regardless of some rather peculiar arguments, nuclear weapons are not the successful manifestation of non-violent beliefs.

When these forces emerge, they are the expression of uncountable forces within an organization. Like Hillis' evolved programs, this expression is usually not only unexpected, but frequently unintelligible unless we begin to familiarize ourselves with the patterns.

Any organization that survives beyond one generation will have within it emergent behavior that ensures its continuing survival. The traits it takes on will almost certainly go against the stated purpose of the individuals within it. If the organization is not built with the power of emergent behavior, it will die. Genghis Khan built an enormous empire, but all the power derived from himself. Soon after he died, so did the empire.

But in an established organization, the people who rise to the top will only be allowed there because the emergent behavior identified them as capable of expressing the needs of the emergent system. It will channel everything so it all makes sense. People who rise in power with ambitions to finally change an organization soon find out why seemingly ridiculous decisions were made. The reasons are so compelling that everything looks pretty much the same on the outside, regardless of who is on the inside.

The church continued to grow and began to reach a truly massive size in power and numbers. Then their numbers passed another critical point. The emergent pattern changed again. The church divided. The Protestants and the Catholics immediately lay into each other in the bloodiest warring we have ever seen.

This an extraordinary development given that every single individual involved had a crystal clear commandment from the highest possible authority not to kill another human being.

It is the best demonstration I know of the power of emergent behavior to override any command. This is the true cause of the death of millions of people in the past, and the present; and it will continue into the future until we liberate ourselves from this unconscious power.

For the Christian Church, once the critical number of people was passed, instead of being an example of how to live peacefully, it began to send armies to force people to see the light. Violence became the means to the promised gentle end. It quickly became evident that many needed the means applied to them. To some of those outside of organized religion, the church began to look like it was motivated by some power-hungry, hypocritical, self-serving, secretive, and dangerous design.

The emergent system had rebuilt reality in an image that best suited its purposes. Soon, even to challenge this created truth could bring about a death in the name of Christianity. The world created at the height of Christian power is about as far from Christian ideals as is possible.

The first person to bring forward evidence that the earth was not the center of the universe was threatened with death by the church. In truth, the church was not upset that everything might not revolve around the earth, it was upset that it had staked its reputation on having superior knowledge of the universe in all respects and this new knowledge threatened to undo that facade. It seems unlikely that the church really cared whether the earth was the center or not. Like so many in power positions, the first line of defense is usually to discredit the source of unpalatable information. In this case, in exchange for his life, the source was commanded to lie (another sin) in a public arena and say his evidence was wrong and the church was right.

Of course, this didn't work. If we still believed this, all of our space rockets would have missed their target because the mathematics would not work. There was a short period where people thought the sun was a foot wide and was therefore about 40 meters above our heads. The Tower of Babylon doesn't look so foolish in light of beliefs like this.

The influence of emergent behavior is not a unique problem for Christians. Every single human organization that passes the critical number of members will come under its influence. If we remain unconscious of what it is doing, we will continue to witness unfortunate characteristics emerging. Teaching science in a manner that implies it is a superior understanding that supersedes religion, spirituality, or any other beliefs judged as primitive, is just as harmful as the faithful concluding that the idea of evolution is the work of the devil. Just as individual scientists might vigorously deny that they diminish other beliefs, so would many individual priests deny that they create an atmosphere of spiritual arrogance.

In a world of disconnection, very few people really understand the full spectrum of their influence in the world. When the hidden impacts of their actions turn up in some horrible but unrecognizable form, most people feel completely uninvolved. Quite frankly, there is very little going on in the world that you and I are not directly empowering, regardless of whether we love it or hate it. People who remain ignorant of how emergent behavior affects them will never have full control of the consequences of their actions and will continue to be influenced by forces outside their awareness.

Profound wisdom is harbored within religion, but its own unconscious emergent behavior has frequently obscured this fact. This emergent behavior can be seen in action when religious people insist that their interpretation of their sacred scripts reveals a truth that supersedes the truths of all other beliefs (the same suggestion all beliefs make, when under the influence). Because this separates people with different beliefs, it is a disconnecting force. Sometimes a feedback loop emerges where the holy interpretation creates the authority to make more holy interpretation that creates more authority…and on it goes. All belief systems that I am aware of have within them a similar ascending pattern of self-empowering authority.

As the understandings in the worldwide society change and grow, the antagonism of the people expressing this emergent behavior grows ever more intense. Where this emergent behavior has the greatest control, religion can set itself up to be an enemy of any knowledge contradicting its holy interpretation of the holy scripts. Many of these interpretations were made hundreds of years ago, and society's growing body of experience and knowledge can seem like taunts to this emergent behavior. This is a powerful separating force in our world that can frequently become lethal.

As humankind learns astonishing things about the world around us, whole sectors of people have found themselves forced to choose between faith and sectarian knowledge. Some who chose religion have had to turn way from sectarian knowledge in order to keep their faith. A process of isolation begins as these groups vainly attempt to promote the details of an unchanging knowledge base as the highest possible truth. In the gap between these groups and all other beliefs lies a darkness that can become an incubator for soul-wrenching unrest.

If religion does not gain control of its own unconscious emergent behavior, it will continue to generate groups whose teachings will fall further and further behind what the rest of us experience as reality, creating an ever deepening darkness between some if its teachings and reality. People who are searching for a safe haven for a version of reality far away from the rest of us frequently find a home in this darkness. This is a very dangerous disconnection. This is why the murderous acts of many radical people hail from religions. People are killed in several countries all over the world as these dynamics continually spawn isolated fringe groups determined to make their unalterable holy point in the blood of others.

New knowledge that supersedes old does not need to be the enemy of religion, even if the old was written. Knowledge has rarely, if ever, superseded the true precious wisdom held within religion or any other belief.

When it eventually came to be accepted that the earth did indeed revolve around the sun, Christianity did not fail the way it feared it would. In fact, people all over the world stand by their faith in spite of the fact that we routinely discover things about reality that directly contradict older "facts" previously taught by their faith.

Every group on earth will need to eventually tackle their own unconscious emergent behavior if we want to heal these gaps, begin the process of connecting again, and be released to find our own destiny. If we could take control of our own emergent behavior in order to heal these gaps, some of today's most divisive arguments might simply vanish. For example, evolution has long been a point of disconnection between creationists and scientists. If we can allow ourselves to open our beliefs, even something that has been as divisive as evolution could transformed into a unifying concept for beliefs.

Do you think we are ready to step onto the staging point where religion, spirituality, and science all meet as equal partners?

The Continuous Consciousness

This is a difficult subject, so in order to be as clear a possible, initially I am going stay as close to the science line of thought as I can. If you are strongly spiritual or religious, you might find this a difficult trek, but I think the destination might please you.

Everyone knows that there is no single cell that is you. By this I mean that I could not take out one cell that contains all your thoughts and feelings and put it in another body and have that be you. If it is not one cell, then how many would I need? Several? Several billion? Your brain? If it is your brain, then what happens if I take a few thousands cells out of it, as happens every time someone gets drunk? Obviously, your personality does not require your entire brain. So how many cells from your brain do I need to contain you? How much does your nervous system contribute to your awareness? What about your memories or your hormones?

Where does one draw the line?

As far as the seat of consciousness is concerned, all these defined groups are arbitrary. An argument could be made for all parts of your body. It would make as much sense if I declared that your glands are where your personality resides because changing your hormones changes your personality.

There is a well known scientist who has identified a phenomenon that he calls the discontinuous mind. It occurs when we use the power of definition to break up continuous systems, like life.

People are always carving up the world in arbitrary lines for the purposes of definition. For example, when does an egg and a sperm become a human being? Immediately after conception? This is when the genes of the two parents combine. Those saying that life begins when the genes combine acknowledge the power of genes. We command genes in a laboratory. Do we command life then? Were not the egg and sperm alive before that? Didn't they have human genes within them? Does anyone suggest that cells that are independently alive and containing human genes, which were released through the natural process of the human body, are not human enough to be considered human? So how many cells does it take to be human? Can't be one, or your hair would be human and a haircut would be murder. But then, isn't an embryo one cell? If we managed to take a stem cell, put a full sequence of human DNA in it and grow it in a womb to make a human, when would it be defined as human? As soon as it had the full human code in it? Well, there are billions of stem cells in your body with the full code in them; should they all be human by the law?

Perhaps it should be only after cells have developed into a fetus. But when is that? When it is two cells? Fours weeks? Four months? When it is born, as many spiritual systems suggest?

If you force someone to make a decision here, it will be completely arbitrary and almost certainly designed to service some belief. What would happen if we decided that human cells are always human and therefore there is no point in which eggs and sperm are not human? This will never be adopted because it destroys the ability of people to announce when something has become an independent human with rights protected by law. Those who want the law need the definition and so the discontinuous mind swings into action.

The result is that we no longer consider ourselves a continuous line of living beings. We have separated ourselves from one another and the entire living world in a way that has created a deep loneliness. The loneliness created by this artificial disconnection may be one of the biggest lies in which we have ever participated.

If we look at any living body, we can witness different levels of life arising everywhere. For example, our bodies harbor bacteria without which we could not live. These bacteria are not us; they have life in their own right. Each cell in our body has a life of its own. Collectively, these cells can have additional identities. There is a kidney, easily defined and separated from our bodies. We are a walking stack of all kinds of different levels of life within us. All these different levels of life can be kept alive in the right conditions if they are removed from our bodies. A single cell, a single organ, an arm or leg, an entire body can all be kept alive pretty much indefinitely. So where does the individual identity of a cell begin and end and where do we begin and end?

If you were to spend the time to study this, these lines would completely blur before your eyes. This is not easily understood because people naturally search for definitive answers. It is a problem. The answer to the question of definition is really there is no real definition. What we call definition is something humans have invented, usually to support whatever belief is dominant at the time.

The point is that there are no lines drawn up in all these millions of different levels of life. Because we cannot in truth draw lines, there is no cell, no group of cells, and no organ where your personality resides. Your personality is the result of everything happening in your body right now.

This is beneficial emergent behavior in action. The activity is not the sum of the activity of any arbitrary group, like your cells. The force of emergent behavior exerts itself all throughout the different levels of your different parts. There are so many aspects to your body, none of them neatly differentiated, that there are emergent behaviors stemming from the myriad of little emergences. If we have the incomprehensible emerge from Hillis' simple number sorting program, the mind boggling possibilities that could result from everything going on inside your body is simply...there are no words. It might even seem supernatural to those who do not understand the workings of emergent behavior.

It can seem supernatural even when we do.

Is it so hard to conceive that such a process might produce a complex personality? Or an identity? Or self-awareness?

Boundaries are almost always artificially created in order for us to better grasp certain principles. We use man-made boundaries as a way to enhance our ability to perceive and understand our surroundings.

Life has varying degrees of ability to sense its surroundings. Viruses have almost none. What they do is wait until they are in the presence of machinery that can reproduce DNA. When that occurs, they chemically reprogram the factory to make their own DNA. That is all they do. They need no awareness whatsoever. Emergent behavior takes care of all the rest. Those that survive more than one generation are likely to survive more and are therefore necessarily made up in such a way to ensure survival. That is how easy it is when you allow the power of emergent behavior to help.

Now, some organisms found they had a better chance of survival if they could resist reprogramming. But in order to do this they needed to become aware of the presence of a hostile virus. At this point, I could easily wield my discontinuous mind right now and claim this is where the awareness race began. But that would create a disconnection in the process of life, so I won't.

The principles of emergent behavior was the mechanism used to begin the organization necessary to increase awareness. Of course, viruses that stumbled on a way to fool the new and growing awareness of the DNA factories became more successful. It was thus that the arms race began.

(Did you notice my discontinuous mind in action in the last sentence?)

To explain every level of evolution would take an enormous book, but very briefly, bacteria are vastly complex machines compared to viruses, capable of feats that even today only bacteria can accomplish. Bacteria eventually stumbled upon the fact that if different bacteria did different things, the potential of the whole group increased. It was bacteria, not Ford, who initiated factories based on division of labor. They have also invented the wheel. It was the principles of emergent behavior that actually gave them the power, the same way it nudged Hillis' little random programs to become expert number counters, it was pushing life to become expert survivalists.

As the bacteria became more dependent on each other, they eventually combined permanently to become a cell. Virus-like life forms are the likely originators of DNA. Bacteria provided the cell. Every cell in your body is made up of elements of these two main life forms. Even today, some things that look like cells are actually cooperating bacteria. There is one cell that still hosts bacteria that have become specialized in using their tail to swim. What is fascinating is that there are many such bacteria lining the sides of the cell and each must move in cooperation with other bacteria up and down the cell. They do this with no communication. In other words, they are using the power of emergent behavior to coordinate movement.

So cells, were already the most complex life form at the time. A new level of self-organization allowed them to became super-organisms!

All the time, increasing awareness is possible because of increasing complexity. Emergent behavior drives them on to become better and better at surviving. Soon cells learn to cooperate and the next thing we know, we get multi-celled organisms. Now the building blocks are in place to a massive leap forward in potential awareness.

The life race leapt forward with great urgency. Living beings sprung eyes and ears. They developed touch and memory. They began to grow internal organs and weapons. They got much more complex and their awareness grew exponentially.

Complex systems make sudden leaps as the number of participating agents passes certain levels. The advantage of building living beings out of cells was that literally billions of them could be joined together in one enormous super-organism. Don't be fooled into thinking it is only our brain. It is a remarkable organ which has its own emergent system made up of a massively complex network of neurons, but almost all animals have one. Some of them are bigger than ours. The sperm whale has the biggest brain in the world. Some scientists argue that Neanderthal's brain was bigger in certain key areas than other humans living at the same time, and yet it was the Neanderthals that became extinct. The brain is only part of the equation.

Our ability to become aware is a function of emergent behavior. This inconceivably complex matrix of life was using the same power that baffled Hillis but on a monumental scale. Life became not only aware of its surroundings, but it became self-aware. Once this happened, the principles of feedback could come into play in consciousness. Now we have super-awareness.

This awareness stemmed from every single part of our bodies. As we learned that there really is not separation within ourselves, only differentiation, every part of ourselves is aware in its own way. But the awareness of ourselves absolutely dwarfs the awareness of the individual cells and bacteria and DNA that make us up.

That was quite a trip. But we are only part way there.

One must realize that the lines of communication within a complex organism are not directly traceable. While our individual cells have the potential to communicate to any cell next to them, they cannot shout. Your gall bladder cannot directly communicate to your toenails. Your nerves operate on a cell by cell basis, even though to us it seems to be a direct line from touch to feeling it. These lines of communication are simply cells specializing in communication. Any cell could do it if it decided to form itself that way. But, again, emergent behavior works its magic.

Consider a stem cell, the blank cell the body makes that can turn itself into any cell in the body. Stem cells must read from the identical set of DNA instructions (except for where DNA has been damaged or mutated) that every single cell in your body contains. This DNA contains the code for every type of cell in your body. If this cell resides in your nose, for example, how does it know to read the part of the DNA sequence that explains how to be a nose cell? Why not a liver cell or a white blood cell?

It used that same mechanism that the economy uses to coax free willed people to choose vocations that naturally maintain the integrity of the economy. Isn't it amazing how the people just happen to choose the right job (through free will) so that the economy continues to thrive? It is the principles of emergent behavior that create this remarkable pattern, just as it creates flows on the pavement. Using the same principles, cells are gently guided to become the cell that is needed the most in the right place. It is all automatic and there is no awareness or consciousness required. We can reproduce these actions on a computer using the principles of emergent behavior.

For a long time, no one believed in radiation or radio waves. Radiation is a spectrum of light that we cannot see. In fact, there are more frequencies of light that are invisible to us than we can see. We can only "prove" their existence by using instruments. If someone chooses to believe only in the light we can see there really isn't anything we can do to convince them otherwise. So, how would life look like to us if we couldn't see it, touch it, or use only our physical senses to detect it? It would almost certainly be very different to anything we know.

So, assuming that the manifestation of consciousness does not stop conveniently at the level that we happen to recognize it, what about a group of animals? If there were enough of them, would the group take on some sort of emergent consciousness? We already know that ant nests can act very much like single living entities. But life is much more varied than that. Again, the kind of life that we most identify with (intelligent mammals) is not necessarily the only way awareness manifests. What about awareness that does not appear in a form we recognize?

There are those who believe that an animal species has a consciousness of its own. What that would mean is that the consciousness of the entire species of salmon, for example, would have an awareness that stems from connections of all the salmon in all the oceans. This awareness would be very different from anything we have known previously because it would not operate in the same time spans that we are used to. While our cells can communicate in a cascade lasting fractions of a second, a salmon cascade might take hours, days, perhaps even weeks.

The principles of emergent behavior are not time dependent, they are change dependent only. If the changes within the individual units occur on the right scale relative to their communication with other units, we will find that the principles of emergent behavior will exert themselves.

So, while there is no immediate proof that I can present, the principles that lead to our consciousness could very well lead to the consciousness of any species with a large enough number. What about the world? It is almost inevitable that everything on earth will be generating an awareness of some sort. There are billions and billions of living things residing here. There are far more than most people realize. There is evidence to suggest that there might be more living matter living off the heat from the lava (probably, but not necessarily, confined to bacteria) than live on top of the earth from the energy of the sunlight.

If all these processes were linked in a way that we cannot easily perceive, it would have the potential to create an enormous awareness. Some of those who feel they can already sense something call it Gaia.

None of this proves that Gaia exists. However, as we demonstrate, life is prone to link itself in these seemingly magical ways to create the many levels of awareness inhabiting our everyday world. This is the same mechanism that evolutionists insist, and have demonstrated, must occur in nature in order to create the magic of evolution. Given all this evidence, then how could something like Gaia not emerge?

We have to be careful in what we conclude here. Just because something has awareness does not mean it is "higher" than our own consciousness. Even though Gaia would be aware of all of the earth at some level, it does not necessarily make it kind, good or even intelligent, anymore than mankind as a whole appears to be acting intelligently. Its values might be so foreign to us that they become meaningless to us.

On the other hand, perhaps Gaia might build on our awareness, and that of every other living thing on earth, to create a huge awareness of exactly the kind that some people hope is there. In the last section of this book, we shall look at an argument as to why Gaia is likely to be this way.

Of course, we are not stopping here. In order to get to the point, we will skip over many different levels of possible consciousness to finally arrive at the entire universe. What could possibly emerge from everything in the universe?

Well, now we run into a technical problem. Information cannot travel faster than the speed of light, so for information to travel from one side of the universe to the other, it would take up a large portion of the entire time the universe has been in existence. As such, emergent awareness is unlikely to form because the different parts would be unable to communicate in a meaningful manner. Another problem (for us) is that even if these far flung parts formed an awareness, its thinking process would be so slow that to us it might as well not exist. Just as the entire lifetime of some subatomic particles lasts mere fractions of a second, so our whole civilization could appear to last a fraction of a second to such a consciousness. All bad. Even if there is some huge God awareness out there, we would not even rate a single thought because we don't live long enough.

This would be true if the whole universe operated the same way that it does for us. However, if we include everything in the universe from all time, we are likely to pass over a critical point, or two. We know that when we pass critical point, it can completely change the characteristics of a system.

In quantum physics, Einstein's equations predict something that is popularly called a worm hole. They are not huge great things that you can put a ship through, as they have been depicted in science fiction work, but brief openings with only enough integrity to transport information. We now have a means for disparate parts of the universe to communicate, one of the keys for awareness to form based on the entire fabric of the universe and possibly at a relevant timescale to us. Also, the ability of different parts of the universe to "shout" to other parts is a far more efficient way of communicating than exists in our bodies. This is a substantial leap in complexity, and therefore the potential, of such an emerged consciousness.

A good way to get a sense of the relative awareness between a possible God awareness and our consciousness is to look at ourselves. Our cells have life and reproduce but compared to us their awareness is very limited. Even though our awareness is made up from the emergent behavior of cells, our cells would never be able to comprehend our awareness. It is so huge that it is rendered meaningless to the cell, even though the fate of the cell might be directly affected by our conscious decisions (getting drunk, getting pregnant, having a tumor removed, etc).

Another characteristic of passing critical points might be that a God consciousness would be likely to take on forms of awareness that are completely outside our ability to even conceive or perceive. For example, while we are not aware of the life and death of our own individual cells, the God awareness might be.

So what would this God thing look like? Well, there would be no physical body in any way we are familiar with. Every single one of us would be part of God but not God itself. Every single one of us would have a tiny bit of God consciousness in us and we would be linked with God, as we must be for emergent behavior to occur. Its consciousness and desires would be so far outside our ability to perceive or conceive that it would be impossible to accurately describe. We simply wouldn't have the faculties to understand.

However, if we are linked then there must be a way to tap into the God consciousness. If all this is true, then perhaps religions do have something to contribute. Isn't it interesting that after millions of years of evolution we find that, according to science, believing in God makes us happier? This might be an aberration of evolution, but the truth is that if you fully understand the forces of evolution then it is irrational to discount the possibility of a God, because God-like consciousness would almost certainly emerge through the very same principles. Not only that, what is likely to occur from our understanding of emergent behavior is exactly what the religions and spiritualists have been saying is there all along.

The magical thing is that just because we are capable of understanding the principles does not mean that the resulting God would be anywhere near our ability to understand. We can't even understand simple little counting programs derived through a few minutes of evolution in a computer. Where would the limits be for an emergent system using literally everything in the existence for as long as the Universe has existed?

The Emergence of Us

I believe that we have the potential to make shifts in human reality that would unlock an unbelievable potential. One the other hand, while we remain unaware of our own emergent behavior, it does not matter how knowledgeable or intelligent we become as individuals. Our destiny will remain a matter of chance. We will be yet one more species on earth blindly following whatever paths we unconsciously plough for ourselves.

Human society has gone through a tremendous transformation in the last fifty years or so. Before this time, our different cultures and beliefs were relatively isolated, struggling with their neighbors to maintain or extend their influence. Divided by culture and beliefs, each pocket of humanity tried a number of ways to survive. The most common survival mechanism was to maintain a strong military. Those that fell behind suffered a fate similar to that of the Palestinians today. Societies all over the world honored powerful military figures because they ensured their people remained safe from incursions of numerous other cultures and beliefs.

As travel became easier, the empires grew larger. This encouraged the most aggressive and dominating cultures to spread their influence, eventually linking the whole world. It exerted a homogenizing force throughout human societies, unconsciously removing a huge amount of wisdom carried in other cultures and beliefs.

A number of functioning societies (and animals and ecologies) have been pressured completely out of existence. The dominant emergent behavior now rules the world even if different cultures disguise the similarities.

The seeds of this new empire were planted by the society that won the survival-of-the-fittest contest that has been recently waged across the world. How could the result be anything other than a dominating force?

As the seed for our worldwide society, these characteristics were deeply embedded in the unconscious imperatives now motivating our emergent behavior. The code words are everywhere. Competitive advantage, market penetration, war on terror, pre-emptive strikes, guilt and innocence (in some cultures crime was so unknown that there were no words in their language to describe guilt) are among the fighting words in our society today. In spite of the cries for peace, our emergent behavior remains on guard in martial readiness, prepared to move against any threat, real or imagined, internal or external.

Recently, there has been another enormous shift in the potential of humankind. Through the computer and the internet, mobile/cell phones and cameras, human beings from across the world are suddenly linked as we never have been before. Even those without technology are affected because one can never be too far from an information output point. The numbers have changed so the character and potential of our emergent behavior has changed as well. It has brought about a tremendous opportunity. For the first time in known history, we have the ability to fully grasp the reins of human emergent behavior and have it become whatever we want it be.

Previously this was not possible. Cultures that worked to harness the power of nature to develop long-term benefits were wiped out anytime a culture intoxicated by short-term power found them. This is inevitable because a culture trying to find balance with life will inevitably create an oasis of resources; just the thing a ravenous sprinter needs to keep on sprinting.

As the sprinting culture begins to tire, the baton is taken (usually be force) by another younger and more vigorous sprinting culture. It looks to me that the United States might be beginning to show signs of fatigue. One of the possible signs is that its stance has shifted from a position of confidence to one of violent defensiveness. At some time in the future, if nothing significantly changes, the United States will be overtaken by a fresh sprinting culture or organization. Then the dice will be thrown again. Will the new leader have the qualities closer to Hitler or Gandhi, something in between, or possibly something we have never seen before?

There is one thing for certain. Barring any changes, the winner will be another ravenous sprinter.

We have a choice. Either we continue to allow the baton to be passed or we could make the shift necessary to reclaim the power to steer our own destiny. The great worldwide unconsciousness could become conscious. The potential of these sprinting cultures will pale in comparison to the realities that could become available to us.

The more time you spend looking at emergent behavior the more obvious its presence becomes. Even those with natural aptitude will become progressively more aware as they experience more of life. That is why cultures that have successfully used emergent behavior to enhance their lives look to their elders for wisdom. The elders' growing sense of the huge patterns around them becomes an invaluable asset. For this to happen, people must learn to seek out these patterns. Being old is not in itself a passport to wisdom.

This is not the same challenge that faced successful indigenous cultures. Numbers change everything. While indigenous cultures have successfully climbed an enormous peak and embraced some very deep understandings of the workings of emergent behavior, it was not conscious enough for them to be aware of emergent behavior at all its levels, especially as their numbers grew.

The entire world is linked now. The forces are complex and insistent. We know local reality is different from global reality so even though we may be linked as never before globally, locally we are creating a frightening pattern of personal isolation. There are several "western" problems emerging in all of the world as a result. I don't think that the internet would have become so widely used if people were more rooted in their own local community. It seems to me that local bonds are fragmenting in favor of disparate global bonds.

The problem with this is that different groups of people are springing up, each looking for a way to express themselves against the pressures of the dominant emergent behavior, sometimes violently. In fact, there is enough noise in the worldwide human society to possibly indicate that we might be at the cusp of a significant change in all of society. If this is true, it could be very dangerous to leave this to chance.

One of the things the great unconscious has done is to set our different belief systems against one another. If we can learn to bring all our beliefs together in conversation we have the potential to make a major leap in the state of human awareness. The first step is to accept that perhaps there is more to reality than any single belief system can deliver. This includes science.

The example of the Jarawa surviving the tsunami is easy to see. However, as was demonstrated by one British schoolgirl, learning to recognize the scientific signs of a tsunami was just as effective. The two belief systems accomplished exactly the same thing using two completely different paths. However, just because science has discovered a similar understanding as an ancient spiritual belief system doesn't mean that it understands all the wisdom in all the different beliefs. In fact, there may be things understood spiritually or religiously that cannot be understood scientifically. Science is simply another filter on reality that reveals what it is good at revealing and disregards the rest. It is no more complete than the faiths that preceded it.

Using different lenses for different purposes opens up all sorts of possibilities. Using a different lens does not invalidate other lenses.

When they were first mapping the ocean floor just after the Second World War, the only lens they had available was sonar. The sonar units were placed on ships traveling slowly across the ocean, bouncing sound off the seabed to measure the depth. This created hundreds of accurate depth lines across the ocean, while 99% of the ocean floor remained unmapped by any direct means. The ocean was simply too vast. The experts had to join the lines and use intelligent guessing to create a map. At the time, the theory of plate tectonic was being fiercely debated. Only fifty years before, people thought earthquakes resulted from God shaking the ground. So when a trench seemed to show up in the middle of the Atlantic, one looking exactly like that which would be required if the theory of plate tectonics was correct, the accuracy of these intelligent guesses took on huge significance.

Running ships across every part of the ocean floor would have taken centuries because that lens is simply inadequate to the task. However, as the debate heated up, they decided to go to the expense of using a different lens. They moved the lens to space and took pictures from satellites. Within a very short time the entire floor of the Atlantic had been accurately pictured. There was indeed a trench. This did not end the debate, but it was the beginning of the end.

But satellite technology did not diminish the effectiveness of sonar. Today, it is still one of the best tools available to explore deep water wrecks. Bouncing sound off the bottom can create extraordinarily detailed images of anything on the ocean floor, even if the depth is far too great for human descent.

Using the right lens for any given task greatly enhances our abilities. Insisting your belief is the only one needed for all of reality cuts off the possibility of using more efficient lenses for certain tasks and disconnects you from any reality that your lens cannot see. For humankind to find a better peak, possibly one that is rising on its own accord, we need to become aware of the combined picture of all the different beliefs in the world. Easy to say, but how would we do it?

Unfortunately for this book, this is much harder to describe in some globally truthful sense than it is to simply to do it. I don't really see a way to say anything that would be acceptable to everyone's belief system as things stand today. It would be much easier for us to get together as we can and see if we can increase our connections.

However, for the sake of completeness, I will attempt to describe a general path that would begin the process. At the back of this book, I describe in detail my own path if anyone wants to view one person's journey.

First of all, hold on to whatever it is you believe in. Whenever reality challenges your belief through either events or a person, at whatever speed is comfortable for you, test it. For example, some people feel their belief will save them from harm. Do people who believe as you do remain safe? If they do get hurt, there are two possibilities (using my discontinuous mind to artificially make definitions). One, they were faulty in their belief so you are still safe or two, they were not faulty and the belief is wrong. Only you can really decide on the answer here, but you must be open to honestly ask some difficult questions of your belief.

If you never find any opening for growth in your beliefs then you are not looking very hard, because no belief holds all of reality.

Fortunately, as we increase our ability to determine our own destiny, the emergent patterns will help us in creating an open atmosphere. The enormous power that can create incomprehensible but effective number sorting solutions can also work for us in creating a completely different level of awareness.

I'm sorry that I am not going to be able to honestly say that after reading this book, all you have to do is a+b+c and then everything will be all right. Personally, I get suspicious of people who suggest it is that easy. For one thing, it suggests that the rest of us are stupid for not figuring it out already.

On the other hand, all the principles in this book are easy to express once you are familiar with them, but if you are not, just like so many things in life, it can seem to be a maze of complexity. However, as difficult as it may seem to grasp the principles, when it clicks into place you will be amazed by the magical connections that suddenly appear to you in the world.

I truly believe that if we do choose to take this path, human existence could go to an entirely different level. We will experience profound connections that only a few people are lucky enough to experience today.

I hope that I have convinced you that the effort to help us all to get there is worth it.

More Detailed Scientific Explanations

Introduction

While we will be looking at some science in more detail, any part of this could be expanded into a work in its own right. There is such a richness of work in all these areas that I feel I need to apologies for giving them such a brief overview.

On the other hand, I am hoping that people exploring these issues on their own will come to understand things I missed. This way we can expand everything.

The internet is an incredible resource. A quick search will probably bring you pages and pages of work on any of these topics. There are several very good books as well, a few of which I have mentioned at the end.

This chapter is devoted to some scientific elements that contribute to the understanding of emergent behavior. What it is not is a scientific presentation. If you are a scientist you will likely be dismayed at my loose use of scientific terms, such as emergent behavior, for example. But this is not intended to be a science book and there has been no attempt to adhere to scientific conventions. I am only using science as a tool for understanding, not in an attempt to imitate scientific rigor. Such rigor is not useful unless the mind has been trained for it.

Ideas throughout this book, including those in this section, are sometimes mixed with non-scientific concepts, as they must be to maintain connections with everything.

The Rise and Fall of Tit for Tat

Previous chapters have suggested that if we could re-wire our own world-wide emergent system everyone would experience a significant increase in life satisfaction, even those who count among the richest and most powerful in society today. This chapter explores the mechanisms that would allow this to happen.

Test readers have indicated that this chapter is hard work for people who are not scientifically minded. If you do not want to know how systems, like our society, can make shifts from a low state to a much higher state without changes to the basic internal workings, then you do not need to read this.

For those who do, this is fascinating research.

The prisoner's dilemma was originally described in 1950 by Merrill Flood and Melvin Dresher as a tool to better understand the behavior of a prisoner who is asked to give evidence against another prisoner in exchange for a reduced sentence. It turned out to be so useful that sociologists quickly adapted it to be used as a general tool for understanding general human behavior. It shows how cooperation can evolve and also how entire societies can become trapped in a very low state compared to what is possible. It also give us clues of how to organize a group or society to attain a very rewarding outcome for everyone.

The prisoner's dilemma begins with two people. Their interaction is limited to displaying a card with two choices; cooperate or deviate. The two players do this at the same time without being allowed to give any clues as to what they are about to play.

If you deviate, you receive one of two possible rewards depending on what the other player did. You will get 5 if they cooperated and you will get 1 if they deviated. If you cooperated, the two possible scores are -1 or 3.

Both players receive their score simultaneously.

		PLAYER A			
		Cooperate		Deviate	
PLAYER B	Cooperate	A: +3	B: +3	A: +5	B: -1
	Deviate	A: -1	B: +5	A: +1	B: +1

The highest score one person can obtain is a five, which requires the opponent to cooperate while you deviate. To accumulate the highest total score, common sense would seem to dictate that you try to trick your opponent into cooperating while you deviate and capture the highest score. Cooperating is unsafe because it makes you vulnerable to your opponent deviating, so this could be tricky. When real people played the prisoner's dilemma, the game frequently stabilized to round after round of deviation by both sides.

Social scientists had been studying the prisoner's dilemma for years, but with the advent of cheap powerful computers, an entirely new realm of exploration was made available. A man named Robert Axelrod created a computer environment governed by the prisoner's dilemma rules. In this environment, a program encountering another program would have a choice of either deviation or cooperation and the environment would keep track of the score for each program. Axelrod then put out a challenge to established game theorists to create a program to compete against the other entries in the prisoner's dilemma environment.

Loosely speaking, there were two strategies. Programs referred to as cooperators tried to capitalize on engaging in successive rounds of the 3 point interactions. The theory here is that cooperators finding other cooperators will do much better even if they are deviated against by more aggressive programs. In the following examples I am going to be calling all programs that tended towards cooperation as cooperators or cooperative programs.

This was expected by other programmers. They programmed devious little beasts that would prowl around looking for ways to catch other programs out and so yield up the precious 5 score. Some of these programs were quite complex, with abilities to track other programs and utilize powerful mathematics to try to predict their behavior and thus take advantage of them. The most complex and sophisticated programs tended towards deviation. In the following examples I am going to call all programs that tried to capture the 5 score as deviators or deviant programs.

This deviator and cooperator split is not as neat as I am presenting it. In actuality, many programs had elements of both in their programming. If you want all the detail, it is readily available both in books (some listed at the back) and on the internet.

The simplest program of them all was called Tit For Tat. Its behavior was completely predictable. On the first meeting it cooperated with everyone and then remembered how it was treated by the other program. The next time it met that program, it did whatever the other program did the last time they met. That was it. Obviously, the deviator programs could read the simple Tit for Tat like a book.

And the winner was…Tit For Tat! The considerable complexity and sophistication of other programs were no match.

To simplify, he deviators did the worst because they frequently ended up engaging in mutual deviation with programs yielding only 1 point per round. The cooperators didn't win because their soft approach allowed the deviators to repeatedly give them negative scores.

Tit for Tat fended off the deviators with the simple means of giving them whatever they dished out. Anytime they deviated, Tit For Tat would deviate right back. The deviator was then faced with a choice. Either it could go round after round of deviation, yielding only 1 point per turn…

Tit For Tat		Deviator	
C	(-1)	D	(5)
D	(1)	D	(1)
D	(1)	D	(1)
D	(1)	D	(1)
D	(1)	D	(1)
D	(1)	D	(1)
D	(1)	D	(1)
D	(1)	D	(1)
Etc.			
Sum	(6)		(12)

System Total (8 turns)   18

…or it had to cooperate to get out of the cycle of deviation. When it cooperated, Tit For Tat would deviate (because that is what the deviating program had done the last time they met) and Tit For Tat would gain back the points lost when the original deviation took place.

Continuing from the last 8 rounds…

Tit For Tat		Deviator	
D	(1)	D	(1)
D	(5)	C	(-1)
C	(3)	C	(3)
C	(3)	C	(3)
C	(3)	C	(3)
C	(3)	C	(3)

C	(3)	C	(3)
C	(3)	C	(3)
Etc.			

Sum	(24)		(18)

System Total (8 turns)   42

Totals for last two rounds (16 turns)

Tit For Tat	Deviator
6+24=30	12+18=30

After that, the deviator could either continue to go through further rounds of cooperating, yielding 3 points a turn, or it could deviate again when it knew Tit For Tat was going to cooperate. It could go round after round of alternating but it would only make 4 every two rounds instead of the possible 6 if they had both cooperated.

Tit For Tat		Deviator	
...			
C	(-1)	D	(5)
D	(5)	C	(-1)
C	(-1)	D	(5)
D	(5)	C	(-1)
C	(-1)	D	(5)
D	(5)	C	(-1)
C	(-1)	D	(5)
D	(5)	C	(-1)
Etc.			

Sum	(12)	(12)

System Total (8 turns)	24

No matter how the deviator tries to manipulate the situation, the maximum number of deviations it can get over on Tit For Tat is one. It can only keep that advantage if it continues to deviate for the rest of its turns.

On the other hand, while the deviators were also finding themselves in mutual deviation rounds with other cooperators, Tit For Tat never did. If you look at the system totals (the points both programs made for each of the 8 turn rounds), they both made significantly more points while they were in the cooperative interactions (the middle set) than any other phase. In the competition, what Tit For Tat did was to maximize its points by reaping the cooperator's reward with other cooperators, while keeping the deviators at bay by immediately and unerringly deviating right back, and thereby keeping its losses to a minimum.

Axelrod published the results and immediately offered a re-match. This time, everyone knew that Tit For Tat, a simple and predictable program, was the one to beat. Some of the best trained minds from both the scientific and corporate community all took aim; Tit For Tat was to go down!

Tit For Tat won again.

There was even an entry called Tit For Two Tats, meaning that it wouldn't respond with deviation until another program had deviated against it twice. The thought behind this was if cooperation was good, more was obviously better. This might seem to be common sense but, as we have seen, systems don't work that way.

This extra gentle version of Tit For Tat was susceptible to the tactic of deviating once and going back to cooperating. Using this method, a deviant program could repeatedly collect the 5 point deviation reward without any retribution. The easiest way to get the most out of Tit For Two Tats is to deviate once (5 points), then cooperate once (3 points) and then repeat.

Tit for Two Tats		Deviator	
C	(-1)	D	(5)
C	(3)	C	(3)
C	(-1)	D	(5)

C	(3)		C	(3)
C	(-1)		D	(5)
C	(3)		C	(3)
C	(-1)		D	(5)
C	(3)		C	(3)
Sum	(8)			(32)

System total (8 turns)   40

Here the deviator does very well indeed. There is a powerful individual incentive to deviate if the system does not have enough safeguards. However, you will notice that over 8 turns the system total is still less than if they had both cooperated.

Not only does too much cheek turning nurture a strong presence of deviation, it contributes to bringing down the whole system.

In this very simple model, it is easy to make the jump from individual reward to a system awareness. Individually, on a single turn, the best move is always to deviate. However, as soon as there are several turns, the best possible move is dependent on how others behave. The best level the system as a whole can attain is one of cooperation, which is completely contrary to the individual rationale that deviating will generate the best single score in any situation (as described on page 32).

Here are all the possibilities for the system as a whole.

Player 1		Player 2		System Total (per turn)
C	(3)	C	(3)	6
C	(-1)	D	(5)	4
D	(5)	C	(-1)	4
D	(1)	D	(1)	2

All this changes again if we add the fascinating element of reproduction. The new rule is that instead of competing only for points, the most successful programs will also be able to reproduce themselves. So, when a program manages a high score relative to other programs, it has the privilege of creating offspring. The goal this time is to see which program can dominate the landscape with its offspring.

Now the game will change into a true system because reproduction introduces feedback. Changes will be continually fed back into the system, allowing for an ebb and flow to develop.

The first new thing that develops is steady states. For example, if you completely populate the environment with deviators and drop in one Tit for Tat program, Tit For Tat will end up behaving exactly like a deviator because that is the only strategy available. If you drop in cheek turning cooperators, the deviators will immediately wipe them out.

However, if you start out with an environment filled with cheek turning cooperators, and you drop in a single deviator program, the deviator will completely wipe out the cooperators and repopulate the environment with deviators. An environment of cheek turning cooperators is not stable.

Sounds bad doesn't it? It is just as we have been told by those who champion the theory of survival of the fittest. Only the strong and ruthless survive. Bring on the testosterone!

Now comes Tit For Tat. Place a deviator in an environment filled with Tit For Tat programs and the deviator will be wiped out. The only survival strategy available to a deviator is to pretend to be a cooperator, lying in wait for something more vulnerable than Tit For Tat to appear.

An environment of Tit for Tats is operating at a 3 point per turn and is very resistant to the encroachment of deviators. An environment of deviators is operating at a 1 point per turn and is resistant to the encroachment of cooperators. An environment of cheek turning cooperators operates at 3 points per turn but is vulnerable to even the slightest hint of deviation. Any deviators present will immediately take over the environment. In system terms, a fully cooperative system has no defense or immunity. But the system will drop from an operating level of 3 points per turn to 1 point per turn. This hurts everyone, including the deviators. But this will only be noticed if the participants have a global awareness.

Only Tit for Tat is robust enough to hold the system in the higher state of averaging close to 3 points per turn for everyone.

While this is fascinating it is not the real world. In order to move to a more realistic model we need to add noise. In the real world, there is imperfect communication and perception. Has anyone you know ever thought you were being nasty or insulting when the thought never crossed your mind? How does the omnipotent Tit For Tat handle things if misunderstandings become a reality?

Well, Tit For Tat is a known anti-deviation agent. It cleans out the environment of many of the deviant programs, but now there is noise, it can't get all of them. Some deviants can thrive within the "noise" in the system. Noise enables them to purposely deviate and gain the deviation payoff undetected. As long as their activity is restrained enough so they don't stand out above the "noise" of misunderstanding there will be no retaliation.

If we run this system, things change. Once Tit For Tat gains a foothold, just like in the noiseless system, it cleans out most of the deviants. However, the noise allows some deviants to remain hidden in the maze of misunderstandings. The more noise there is in the system, the larger and bolder will be the deviants because noise weakens the connection between the programs. High states can only be achieved in an environment of good connections.

But the noise also interferes with the Tit For Tat programs. Sometimes a Tit For Tat program will think it has been deviated against and retaliate in response. If it is against another Tit For Tat program, this will set up an alternating cooperate, deviate cycle which they will remain stuck inside unless lightening strikes twice and "noise" makes them think they both cooperated on a turn when they didn't. One program will deviate on a misunderstanding.

Tit For Tat 1	Tit For Tat 2	
C	C	(but mistakenly believes Tit For Tat 1 deviated against it, so in the next turn...)
C	D	(...Tit For Tat 2 deviates in reality.)
D	C	
C	D	

Pockets of deviating/cooperating Tit for Tats will spring up according to how much noise there is.

Now enters the revenge of Tit for Two Tats. Before Tit For Tat has cleared out most of the dominating programs, Tit for Two Tats has little hope. However, afterwards the environment is much more cooperative and so it can gain a foothold. Because of the noise, Tit for Two Tats does not get stuck in the cycle of alternating deviation to which Tit For Tat is vulnerable. What this means is that Tit for Two Tats will begin to dominate the entire environment.

Tit For Two Tats 1	Tit For Two Tats 2	
C	C	(but mistakenly believes Tit For Two Tats 1 deviated against it, so...)
C	C	(...Tit For Two Tats 2 still cooperates because it will only retaliate after the other program deviates twice. No harm is done.)
C	C	
C	C	

However, this also allows the presence of deviant programs to have limited success.

Deviant	Tit For Two Tats	
D	C	
C	C	
D	C	
C	C	(but noise makes it seem like the Deviant deviated against Tit For Two Tats in this turn as well as last turn so, in the next turn...)
D	D	(...Tit For Two Tats retaliates in this turn)
D	D	

A Tit For Tat program would never allow this to happen, but these "thieves" can only occur in a limited way.

So the new environment contains some deviants, some Tit for Tats (acting almost as policemen), but mainly Tit for Two Tats.

All through these progressions, the total score of the entire environment keeps rising. So even though having Tit For Two Tats dominate allows the deviants to grow in the softer environment, a better overall score is achieved each round than if Tit For Tat dominated.

For those technically minded, if you chart the aggregate score per turn of the entire system over a very high number of cycles, as would be expected of a system containing feedback, it takes on chaotic characteristics. In layman's terms, the level of the system can fluctuate over a long period of time.

It does not end here. Each time the environment changes, there is an opportunity for another evolution in the program. In the experiments done with the prisoner's dilemma environment, all the programs were either present from the beginning or introduced by a programmer. The different phases within the environment created opportunities for different programs. But in nature, there isn't a team of programmers introducing programs, so how does it work in reality?

Each program is simply a way of behaving. Axelrod calls it the strategy. We can change that anytime we want. In society there are certain ways of behaving that will work the best. If a better way is established throughout society, then it opens the door to more opportunities. But without the awareness of our own emergent behavior, we frequently optimize locally and therefore miss out on the large payoff that is possible globally. In other words, our emergent behavior turns us into unknowing deviants.

Some people believe they can describe a way to behave that will create a Utopia, but this is the same idea as trying to command an economy. Society is far more complex than the economy (the economy only being one small part of society, in spite of what some might think) and the force firmly in control is emergent behavior. We simply do not have the awareness or capacity to improve in its ability to balance all the societal forces. Nor would we want to, anymore than we would like to manually take over all our automatic body functions (again, we do not have the awareness or capacity to do so). However, if we come to know the principles of the emergent behavior we can then harness its strengths and begin to move out certain undesirable traits and create more of the good, without taking away anyone's freedom to do as they wish.

Critical Points

Critical points describe the place where a system's characteristics suddenly change. A block of enriched uranium does emit radiation, but it is otherwise unremarkable (except it is every heavy). However, if the mass passes a critical level it will respond in what is commonly known as an atomic explosion. This is considered "going critical".

In emergent behavior, the flows are maintained in a certain way to create certain predictable patterns, but if enough pressure is exerted they will change. For example, if you take ice and heat it, it will suddenly change into water at a critical point. It will remain in this state even though you keep heating it. However, at another critical point, it will turn into vapor.

If you were not familiar with the critical points of water you would be forgiven for making some fundamental mistakes. For example, let us say you were charged with the problem of crossing rivers. You examine the water and discover that by cooling it by only one degree it will suddenly turn solid. Amazing! You run to your commander and declare that all water turns solid if you cool it by one degree.

Because of our familiarity with water's critical points, we know that the water was obviously very close to freezing to begin. So when this group of people end up drowning, we think; you fools, didn't you noticed that the water has to be at a certain temperature to turn solid?

By the way, if you rearrange the atoms you can change this emergent system entirely and get it to freeze at a completely different temperature. The nature of the "individual" is determined by the atomic makeup of the molecule. The resulting emergent behavior is the characteristics of the resulting element. For example, if you took out the oxygen, you would be left with hydrogen, which has an entirely different set of critical points. Chemistry is so powerful because we are directly accessing the key to shifting the emergent behavior of different molecules. It is the same reason that manipulating DNA is so powerful. However, I believe there is a danger here because I don't think people have a deep enough understanding of the emergent behavior of all the life on earth to avoid unintended consequences.

There are many critical points in society and we frequently test only one cup before declaring we know how to create a better society.

For systems made up of people, critical points come in a variety of flavors. For example, people milling around will start to form orderly flows at very distinct levels of density. On a hundred acre grassy field, changing the number of people from five to ten will do absolutely nothing. But at some critical level, adding just a few people will cause the orderly emergent flows to appear.

But society is much more complex than that. In New York, they recently had a stunning success in reducing crime. When asked how they did it, the answer did not seem revolutionary or even overly imaginative. Many city leaders went away scratching their heads trying to figure out the real reason behind New York's success.

It is very possible that New York's emergent flows were poised on the edge of a critical point. By exerting just a little additional pressure, the crime rate snapped to a new stable level. Others trying to duplicate the success will fail because their city is not poised on a same critical point. And yet, common sense suggests that if you do exactly what New York did in another city then the same thing would happen. If only it were that easy.

Critical points can frequently shift in society. Successes are frequently examples of luck rather than superior technique. That is why seemingly effortless successes are rarely duplicated and in spite of our best efforts, significant designed shifts in society are very rare indeed.

Critical points have another trick up their sleeve. They do not always occur at the same point or in the same way in anything, even in something as simple and common as water. It is possible for water to remain liquid below the known freezing level. At these temperatures, it is possible for water to be in one of two states, either solid or liquid, at a given temperature. If water has remained liquid below freezing it is considered to be supercooled. Sometimes, only a slight knock is required for it to snap into a solid state.

As with most things in the world, the line is not drawn quite as neatly as we would like. As the temperature of water drops, it becomes more likely that it will turn to ice and less likely that it will remain liquid. This is a characteristic of critical points. At the boundary layer there is a fuzzy area where one of either two states is equally likely. Sometimes, both states can coexist.

On a busy road, cars act together to create state changes. If the traffic is light, the movements are random, just as are the movements of gas molecules. Cars move at speeds of their choice and move in and out of lanes whenever the mood takes them. However, as more cars come onto the road, there is a critical point where the traffic begins to flow in orderly lines. Everyone's speed in each lane becomes more uniform. People feel more pressure to remain in their lane. This is analogous to water. Then, an accident happens. The traffic stops. Now it is a solid.

Just like water, traffic can remain fluid past the point where density usually solidifies it into a jam. When this happens, it takes very little to make traffic come to a standstill. Even someone braking unexpectedly can be enough to create miles of queues behind them as the traffic reverts to its most likely state at that density.

These critical points occur throughout society and must not be confused with effective policy. The main indicator that an apparent success was a result of being on a critical point is that it is not reproducible except where the situations are identical (the water is the same temperature). We could save a lot of effort and resources if we ceased chasing after these cups of water.

As individuals, we frequently try to emulate the successful. However, because others happened to be on a critical point when they exerted some effort, many followers are left with disappointment. Following in a successful person's path, doing exactly what they were doing, could lead to a completely different outcome. Sometimes reality teases us by holding a critical point in place until a certain number of people have passed through and then moving it.

If everyone graduated from university, they would not have all the same opportunities that those who graduated early in the last century had. Last century, graduating from a university was a relatively rare occurrence. As such, graduates had rare opportunities. As becoming a university graduate becomes more normal, then the opportunities will also become average or normal. Then another yardstick will emerge to seek out extraordinary people.

The most stable and predictable path is always the common path, but it will rarely lead to great success. That is the reward reserved for people taking chances by stepping off the predictable common path and trying new things. When it works, the rewards can be tremendous. However, when it doesn't work, as is the usual case, the losses mount.

At this point, people who love you frequently encourage you to re-enter the normal predictable routes of society. These are, of course, the channels empowered by emergent behavior. People who demand mass access to the same opportunities that seem to differentiate successful people are only creating a new measurement of normality. These differentiations will move long before the masses get there.

The key to creating real and permanent shifts that will bring a real improvement to all our lives is to learn to identify the critical points in the emergent system of society. This alone could allow us to effectively allocate limited resources to make real and reasonably permanent changes.

Systems

A system is any entity that changes over time. Systems can be as simple as the population of deer or as complex as the entire ecological system. The ecosystem is made up of millions of different plants and animals, all of which are fluctuating by the moment. Even something as simple as growing grass can baffle the experts for years before they understand which particular parts of the system are important.

This is a real world example. There was a case where the grasses were dying out in protected grazing lands. This was a potential catastrophe that could wipe out entire ecosystems. If the grass died, the grazing animals would die out, followed quickly by predators. Humankind's vast meat herds were also in danger. We had to save the grass.

What they did was cull the grazing animals. That is common sense, isn't it? If you want the grass to recover, kill off what is eating it. That is the strong point of common sense. Cause and effect.

Well, it did nothing. The grass continued to die off. Luckily, one person who understood the natural systems better than most managed to be heard. What they eventually did was introduce natural predators. It worked. It turned out that people killing off the grazers did not work, while allowing natural predators to kill off the grazers did work.

Without a system awareness, this would seem completely irrational. Perhaps it was magic. Some wondered if the nature gods were at work.

Take a moment to consider how difficult it is to unravel before hindsight is available. Common sense can look quite foolish if the effort is not made to find the crucial elements in a system. These same dynamics can cause tremendous problems with the public when dealing with emotional problems like drug abuse, crime, child abuse, etc.

Sometimes effective solutions are impossible to implement because they are so difficult to understand using common sense that no one will take them seriously. But if people take the time to educate themselves, the answer is obvious. The whole concept of "common sense" can be moved to a completely different and more effective place.

In the grasslands, it turns out that the grass had evolved to take advantage of the situation created by the ancient dance between prey and predator. How not? The predators caused the grazers to bunch up for protection instead of spreading out and uniformly eating huge swathes of grass. So the grazers would tend to stay in one area for a while, largely stripping all the edible ground vegetation. When the predators attacked, the grazers would run off in a soil churning rush. The eaten area now had freshly churned soil, with fresh manure (laced with seeds) for fertilization, and no other vegetative competition shading the ground (because the grazers have eaten them). It was an ideal growing situation for the grass.

See how it all makes sense? In hindsight it is so easily seen. The forces within these systems are so incredibly complex that it can be impossible to determine which of the thousands of factors is the crucial one in a particular case.

It is important to keep in mind that cause and effect move and change in a system. The grass might start dying out again, but perhaps this time it would be caused by an insect whose predators were killed off by pollution. Or maybe it was a disease that got out of balance because of global warming. It could be anything.

The human body is a system. That is why illnesses are so complicated to counter in a logical fashion. Certain symptoms in one person may be caused by something entirely different in another. Doctors frequently deal in probabilities because that is all they can offer. Given all the people they have seen with your symptoms, this is the percentage that got well when they did x. There is no guarantee for anyone.

A school is also a system. It is made up of differing levels of students and teachers who all spend a different amount of money a year in order to churn out, with various degrees of success, "educated" students.

Systems are everywhere and usually they are interlinked which makes them even more complex. A school, for example, can be influenced by many "external" factors such a crime rates, inflation, immigration, technology, the wealth of the parents…the list goes on indefinitely.

One of the least understood elements of systems is just how sensitive they are to everything going on around them. For a long time, many meteorologists thought that a gust of air caused by a cough would simply be absorbed into the weather system. It is simply common sense, isn't it?

In fact, over time, a single cough will substantially change the weather system from what it would have looked like. This is a fascinating paradox. While a system will robustly keep its shape regardless of what an individual does, over time, what any individual does vastly changes all the systems that touched that person.

Scientists call this the sensitive dependence on initial conditions. Feedback is why it happens.

Feedback

If you take a penny and double it you will get one extra penny. So doubling the single penny for thirty days will give you a grand total of 31 pennies (30 + your original penny).

Now, let us introduce feedback. Instead of doubling your initial amount only, now you double the total from the previous day. So the first day you have two pennies, the next you have four, the next you have eight, etc. Instead of 31 pennies, at the end of thirty days you will end up with 1,073,741,824 pennies. This is an explosion of wealth.

This is the same mechanism that makes the atomic bomb go boom.

Feedback introduces enormous forces into any system, in terms of both power and complexity. All the living systems that I am aware of have feedback within them, but if the system as a whole is stable, then that means the different forces of feedback are balancing each other. This is why some systems, like living beings, can die so suddenly when certain parameters are passed. For example, raise the arsenic level in a human and death will be remarkably sudden. A rise in your core temperature will create the same result. By the way, lowering the arsenic level in your body to zero may also kill you.

This complexity is why common sense can fail when dealing with systems. In nature, not only do all the individual systems contain feedback, but the systems interact with other systems in ways that generate multiple layers of feedback as well. Many of the world's systems, living and dead, swirl and engage at so many different changing levels that the results can be mind-boggling to many people.

Over a month, doubling a penny using feedback will turn anyone into a millionaire. That is why even a little puff of wind can completely change how the weather would have looked over time. Every single puff of wind, every single minute change of temperature, every ray of sun bouncing (or not) off a cloud, can become caught up in the great natural feedback system and be amplified millions of times. The expression of the weather over time is the resolution to an infinite number of variables.

Society is also a system. Everything you do can be expressed very loudly at some time in the future. What that means is that your life is part of a great swirl of feedback. Society will be different because you are here. If society is sitting at a critical state, your life might be the one that snaps all of society into an entirely different state.

It was a meteorologist who stumbled upon this. At the time many people believed that our world was linearly deterministic, meaning that if we knew enough about it we could predict exactly what was going to happen. There was a race to find the final set of variables and run it on a sufficiently powerful computer in order to accurately predict the weather many years ahead.

It was Edward Lorenz that demonstrated why accurate long-range forecasts are impossible.

As with many true breakthroughs, it was an accident. He had one of the first small computers available set up in his office on which he ran three equations (twelve variables total) simulating temperature, pressure and wind. In the real world, the pressure influences temperature and winds, so he dutifully arranged the answer of each equation to be fed back into the other two equations on the next turn. While his model had no link with the real weather system, his model did change with tantalizing unpredictability all the while staying within certain ranges. In other words, it acted like the real weather.

Lorenz made simple line charts of the temperature, pressure and wind speed of his artificial weather system. He did different little experiments using his system and one day he decided to restart it in the middle of a run. All he wanted to do was return his system to a certain point to make a study. To do this, he went to the point in his computer print-out where he wanted to restarted the system and inputted the numbers directly into the computer. Since the numbers were the same, and the equations were the same, he expected his system to exactly reproduce his previous chart. He was astonished that his weather system veered wildly from the previous pattern.

Mathematically, his model was made up of three simple equations. Lorenz wondered if something was wrong with the vacuum tubes on his computer. Then he re-examined his numbers to make sure he had not made a mistake. All was well. But then what explained the difference?

What happened was the printout cut off the final decimal places at the end of each number to save space. The difference was a tiny fraction, as if someone sneezed into a storm. At first, Lorenz's weather system did not notice the tiny change. It matched the previous run just as it should have. But then it began to subtly deviate from the first pattern. Soon that deviation grew to an outright contradiction. After a little more time, the first system looked entirely different from the second.

What this meant was that even the slightest change in the variables that make up a system will send it off in an entirely different direction. Living systems include absolutely everything at every level in their expressions. People used to think that all the little things would be swept away to vanish in the larger events of the day. How could a cough in a hurricane change the weather? Well, with the power of feedback, it is actually not only possible, but inevitable.

Lorenz immediately knew that long-term weather prediction would never be possible. If even the tiniest things change the system radically over time, how can anyone possibly gather enough information to make a long-term prediction?

Did you just breathe? We don't know how, but you just changed the future weather. Since everything on earth is linked, you also changed the life systems on this planet. If you allow for all the time in our universe, then you just changed the universe as well.

All with one little breath. Isn't that extraordinary?

By the way, this is why time travel is impossible. Even if time were what many people think it is and we had the technology to travel back, the moment we arrived in the past we would introduce the tiniest variation into the world, even if it is simply one person glancing at a newly introduced faint flash of light. The present we know would immediately be replaced by a completely new reality. We would forever lose our home. (Don't get me wrong, I love Dr Who)

As a matter of accuracy, there are two types of feedback. One automatically brings a system towards a particular point and is called negative feedback. For example, the human body has a system that regulates the temperature of our body, so regardless of outside conditions, it stays pretty much the same. This is good, as human beings die if our core temperature deviates by a few degrees.

Another example of negative feedback is how the moon continues to rotate at exactly the right speed to always face the same way towards the earth, in spite of being occasionally pounded by huge meteors.

The other type, positive feedback, can build on itself to become a massive force. Unchecked positive feedback can crash through just about any stabilizing force and destroy the universe. Luckily, the laws of energy in our universe prevent an unchecked positive feedback explosion.

With our weather, it is negative feedback that holds it to predictable patterns, which is why we know it will be cold in the winter and warm in the summer. Considering the enormous forces involved, our weather is amazingly predictable year after year. By this I mean you don't need to worry about frostbite in the Sahara and you generally don't need to make preparations against heat stroke in Antarctica.

The concern of some people is that global warming might initiate a positive feedback cycle within the weather system that will create a character changing event. Having something as powerful as the weather going through a state change would unleash unimaginable power. The problem is, of course, no one knows if or when this balance will be tipped or what the critical indications might be.

What we do know is the weather system is one of the biggest matches that we have ever lit. If we are fortunate, we might learn quickly enough to avoid burning our house down.

Nodal Points

A node is where things intersect or meet. On a plant, several leaves emerging from one place in the stem is one example of a node. A telephone exchange, where thousands of telephone lines meet, is an example of a system nodal point.

Sometimes (all the time in nature) nodal points are not designed, they simply occur as a result of the forces present. The current architecture of the internet was not designed; it simply occurred as a result the needs of the people using it.

In the 1960s the US government had a problem. Like just about any man-made system, their communication network had a few crucial points on which the integrity of the entire system rested. If a crucial point was knocked out by something like a nuclear strike, their entire communication network would fail. An effective retaliation could not be coordinated. As a result, the United States would not be able to kill off the Soviets (even though many Soviets would likely be killed by the fallout of their own missiles) because they wouldn't be able to get their command out to launch their retaliatory strike. This nightmare scenario had to be averted.

What was needed was a nuclear-proof communication system, one that could absorb the loss of many key junctions and still remain functional. Obviously, a centralized system would be useless because the center would simply become a big bullseye.

The solution turned out to be the architectural model for the internet. They decided to directly link all the computers together so that all computers had the ability to communicate directly with all other computers. Now there was no center. Any time a computer or line was knocked out, the system would automatically find another route. It was extremely robust in the face of all eventualities.

This architecture turned out to be an incredibly useful means of communication. People found they could send messages to one another in a far more efficient way than either the post or the telephone. Another benefit of such a system is that if one path becomes full, the system can simply re-route communication through another less traveled avenue. We don't get busy signals on internet lines the way we do when a telephone lines reaches capacity, because the internet will simply re-route the signal to an open line. This constant re-routing can occasionally produce a very convoluted path which is why some e-mails take a while to arrive. Busy signals only occur on the internet when the computer you are trying to access is unable to respond in a timely fashion, not because the line to the computer becomes clogged as can happen with telephone lines.

As the internet grew it quickly went beyond its original remit and became more and more organic in its nature. Computers were piling on in their millions, simultaneously creating more communication channels. But some computers were more conveniently placed than others. Instead of a completely open system where each computer could communicate equally to all other computers, they started to prefer certain computers to route their communication. As this occurred, more and more traffic tended to channel itself through certain groups of computers. The internet had grown to evolve nodal points.

Nodal points in open systems like the internet (or our bodies) are not as vulnerable as nodal points in a linear system because all the other routes are still available. Nodal points appear because it makes the overall system more efficient. Knocking out these nodal points reduces efficiency but does not stop communication altogether. We could knock out every known nodal point and the internet would simply create more.

The way a system creates these nodal points is through the presence of unequal forces. People acting together also create these "floating" nodal points in several different ways. For example, we like certain people more than others. These people are our close friends. Not only that, but the people in your close knit group are likely to name the same people you consider close friends as their close friends. Thus your circle of friends emerges. This is a nodal point in society.

But this does not mean that this group is all the people you know. There are ties that lead outside it. These link you to other groups, but not as strongly as to the people in your group. The links from group to group span all across society. Though it might not seem like this, it has been demonstrated that we are not more that approximately six people away from anyone in the world.

Society is made up of millions and millions of these distinct groups. But certain groups are more desirable to link with than other groups. As a result, the outside communication lines for the more popular groups tend to be more heavily used. Groups tend to try to get closer to these popular groups. Another set of nodal points forms in society as certain groups become more popular than others. What this means is these more popular groups are good places to channel, manipulate, or introduce information because a nodal point is where the most people eventually pass through. It has become a key point of connection.

If a single nodal point, such as one group of friends, breaks up, it does not destroy the ability for people to connect. Inefficiencies will be introduced into the system even if that group was considered unpopular. The capability of the system as a whole will be reduced unless and until other nodal points form to take up the slack. If that group happened to be an important nodal point for society, the break-up will have a larger impact on the efficiency of communication and it will take longer for the system to recover, but it won't stop it.

This behavior mirrors the nuclear forces in subatomic physics. The strong and weak atomic forces create clumps of subatomic matter which have been identified as atoms. These atoms then clump together in the same way to create molecules. Molecules clump together to make organs and other distinct entities. This can be carried on and on right up until we reach the limit of our current physical perception—galaxies clumping together. What is it we get if we link clumped galaxies together? Is there more than one universe and if so do they clump together as well?

All these clumps make up nodal points at different scales. They are important to emergent behavior because they create points of influence, the same way Chinese traditional medicine tries to manipulate the nodal points on the body in order to bring about a healthy balance. Finding nodal points in society is challenging because while some are stable, there are other ones that are rapidly changing and evolving.

Belief systems are among the most important nodal points in society. Huge swathes of society can be influenced depending on the quality and openness of the beliefs involved. Books could be written on our relationship to beliefs and how they control our perception of reality. Any shift in a major belief will bring about considerable changes in the emergent behavior of society.

Another important set of societal nodal points is our information system. This is like our nervous system. The quality and openness of information at different nodal points will also directly influence the nature of our system, which is why several dictators practice intense censorship. However, if we want the state of humankind to find a higher existence, we need to clean up these nodal points as much a possible. The press of any country used to be a key information nodal point for that country, but now this has been challenged by the internet.

The information nodal points of the internet are still in their infancy and have yet to be reformed by the inevitable influence of emergent behavior (this is a feedback system). What the internet has managed to accomplish is to increase the quality and spread of information nodal points. With a few notable exceptions, one has to be very isolated indeed not to be able to inform oneself about just about any subject one chooses.

If we can learn to identify nodal points in our emergent systems then we could develop a powerful tool to improve our awareness, our society, and the world.

Landscapes, Peaks, and Evolutionary Fitness

If you watch the ocean on a windy day you will see waves. They appear and disappear, rising and falling all over the surface of the water. At any given time, it is a fact that one wave will always be higher than all the rest. But it doesn't stay that way for long. Up it comes and down it goes. It is a very complex and varying environment, impossible to predict.

If you were to slow down the picture to such a degree that the waves were barely moving, then even though the waterscape is factually unchanged, it would now appear to be very stable. The earth's climate, for example, might appear stable to us (basically the same over several years) because of our short lifespan, but actually, it is not. We have been riding on a surprising calm for the last 10,000 years or so. Some believe that this is why humankind has recently flourished. Complexity is best nurtured in a stable environment. The act of global warming is likely to move us out that climatic calm and into the normal turbulent waves of the earth's climate.

There are many things that appear unusually still or unusually turbulent simply because we tend to look at things through only one timescale; our own. That is why the movements of tectonic plates remained invisible to people for so long. The man that first suggested the plates of the earth moved about was soundly ridiculed.

While we sometimes talk about local peaks as though they are fixed, in reality they are not. All of living reality shifts and moves in response to what is going on around. What was once a superb strategy can become old and inefficient. Differing landscapes can change at different speeds and at different times. The landscape of farming was unchanging for hundreds of years and then the landscape radically shifted with the invention of tractors, then chemical fertilizers, and then genetic engineering. The landscape of the stock market can shift in seconds.

Living organisms need some sort of mechanism to survive in the long-run in these shifting sands. Non-evolving beings may have the potential to be dominant for a time, but as soon as their landscape shifts they will slip from their peak. The power generating these shifts is frequently the evolution of other beings.

This is how waves can become truly unpredictable. The feedback of the power of evolution generating waves in a wavy environment generates an totally unpredictable reality, even if it looks stable during certain times.

Now, in all this, the tool that living beings use to hold themselves present in such uncertainty is, paradoxically, evolution. Just like Hillis' number sorting programs, evolution is the tool used by living systems can take into account millions of different factors and make the optimal adaptations at any given time. However, the way evolution seeks out peaks is not straightforward. As is the nature of emergent systems, what can seem to be a local hindrance can turn out to be the key to global success.

With Hillis' number sorting programs, the initial evolutionary force was the greater breeding success of the programs that best sorted the numbers. But there are many methods to sort numbers and some ways have more potential than others. It is the nature of life that there are many more available strategies to succeed in a mediocre fashion than there are routes to become the best. There may be many peaks that might be high relative to their local surroundings, but at any one time, none but one is the highest of them all.

What any evolutionary system does is to start climbing the first thing it finds that goes up. It has no idea whether the base of its slope leads to a mild hill or a towering mountain. Once it gets to the peak of chosen slope, there is nowhere to go but down. So it climbs the first peak it finds and then stays there because any move will cause it to lose height. Unless it is lucky (or unlucky), that peak will be around an average height relative to all the peaks in its environment.

This is exactly what happened to Hillis' evolving number sorting program. Successful reproduction was based on the ability of the number sorters to sort numbers. This worked fine as long as there was potential to develop the method they started with. However, once the potential was exhausted, all the number sorters peaked at the new level. Each new generation of number sorters were only slight variations on the old ones.

In Hillis' computer environment, the number sorters reached a local peak of seventy-five steps and stopped improving. That was no good since the all time record was only sixty steps. But perhaps that was as good as evolution gets.

Hold on a minute. Wasn't there something present in nature that was not present in Hillis' evolutionary system?

Enter the predator.

What he did was to introduce a new program that would hunt down his number counters whenever they stopped at a certain level. What this meant was that the local peak of seventy-five steps was no longer a peak. Predators redefined the waves of the system so that the seventy-five peak became a lowering peak, one that would bring about the death of the number counters if they stayed on it. Like rats on a sinking ship, they fled their comfortable peak to find another higher peak.

The moment Hillis introduced predators, the number sorting programs quickly improved to only sixty-two steps, just two shy of the world record.

There are a couple of interesting points to be made here. First of all, it again demonstrates the weakness of being completely cooperative. It is like being Tit for an Infinite Amount of Tats. As well as being very vulnerable to deviant behavior, it will also limit your ability to climb the peaks. Remember, as stable as they might look, peaks move up and down, and in the long-run it is not an optional lifestyle to bundle oneself up with nothing but supportive cooperation.

That does not mean we always need to have successful predators in our midst. But it does mean that at least some people in our society must keep honing their skills at overcoming challenges, willfully entering and surviving risky situations, pushing the edge. If this were trained, bred or legislated out of humankind, we would be extremely vulnerable to any shift in the peaks.

To finish this section, I would like to relate an experiment done by the social scientists Axelrod and Bennett. They were using computers and landscape theory to attempt to predict the political alliances of countries. What they decided to do was to create very simplistic models of countries in 1936 based on some defined, but arbitrary, information. Well, it wasn't completely arbitrary because these two people were very clever social scientists.

They picked ethnicity, religion, territorial disputes, ideology, economy, and past history. Then they assigned a simple number, 1 or -1, to each of these six factors. For example, if both countries were Catholic then the number of religion between these two countries was 1. If they were in dispute over their borders then the number for territorial disputes was -1.

The researchers also factored in a degree of "power" that country had as calculated by the United States political scientists using six factors of demography and industrial and military strength. They threw all these figures into a computer to map the probability of all the 65,536 different ways the sixteen considered countries could align themselves in World War II.

The probability was important. You see, it was unlikely that all the countries of the world would unite behind the goal of invading Latvia. But the question was; will the computer know this from these inputs? What do you think is the probability of anything realistic coming out of a calculation based on these simplistic assumptions?

Remember what I said about detail vastly altering outcome over time so prediction was useless? These social scientists had thrown out so much detail that their assumptions bore little resemblance to the complexity of reality.

On the other hand, haven't we been exploring how emergent behavior reduces an immense amount of information into predictability if we only knew the keys?

Which force do you think prevailed?

Using the most basic details about the characteristics of countries, even when reducing all the variability to only a 1 or -1, the landscape model accurately predicted the World War II alliances with only two exceptions: Poland and Portugal. What this demonstrated (other than the usefulness of landscape models) is that Bennett and Axelrod had become very adept at picking out the key elements that shape certain areas of the world's emergent behavior. Our capacity in this area is rapidly building.

The reason the detail was unimportant in this model was because there was practically no time. It was an attempt to understand the forces that shaped countries' decisions within a short time in history. It would be a useless model to predict alliances a century from now, because it has no capacity to understand the evolution of countries. Evolution is where the real magic happens.

While some of our tools are remarkably revealing, we must understand their limitations. Science is remarkable for unveiling key nodal points in reality, but only reality itself has all the information we need. There are some things that science will never know. For example, what has emerged from everything in the universe after billions of years? Science is simply the wrong tool. For this, we need to pick something that is more apt at accurately expressing the state of uncountable pieces of information. This is where the religious and spiritual lenses can take up the slack.

Still, science is fascinating and has a great contribution to make towards the making of the staging points we use to venture out to other beliefs.

Wild Conjectures

This is where I part company from the big picture and tell you what I see looking through my own lens. There are no great efforts in this section to validate other lenses or even to validate my own. I will be writing as if my lens is true, even though we both know there is more to reality than that. Walk in these pages at your own risk.

The Time Consciousness

We usually measure speed against the apparent stillness of the earth, even though the earth is itself hurtling across space at a phenomenal rate relative to the center of the galaxy. Our galaxy is hurtling though space relative to other galaxies. As Einstein explained, there are no absolute references for speed.

There are no absolute references for time, either. Any change that takes place must be measured against the changes around it in order to create a context. Some take milliseconds while others take millions of years. It is just the way it is.

Being human, we tend to think of changes relative to our life. If a cycle takes longer than one human life, then it is long lived and visa versa. So a thousand year old tree is old, but a fly that lives a couple of days must have a short life. But do we really understand the full level of changes going on inside their world?

If something cycles more quickly than we do, even if it lives a shorter life than we do, it may actually experience what feels like a longer and richer life than we do. Of course, something that has remained almost unchanged for a thousand years might be very young and inexperienced, because consciousness and evolution are cycle dependent. It is not time dependent because time does not link us in any way. No absolute time scale exists from which to measure anything, just as there is no absolute speed from which to measure the speed of anything.

Different processes occur at different time scales. Geologists think of time in millions of years because that is the timescale needed to measure meaningful changes in this field. In subatomic physics, time is measure in nanoseconds (or smaller), because that is the time you need to detect meaningful changes. In many instances in subatomic physics, that is all the time that something even exists.

For example, the movement of tectonic plates follows the rules of fluids. In other words, the earth's crust would appear liquid to us if our lives cycled at a different slower speed. It looks solid to us because the fluid movement of the plates takes so much time relative to our life that nothing, except an occasional rumble, happens in a single lifetime. Compared to plates we are flashes of energy that sparkle all over the earth. If a tectonic plate had consciousness, it would never consider that a human had any progressive or measurable changes, because our lives would last a mere moment relative to its experience.

In the film industry, when they want to indicate a stoppage of time they show clocks that have stopped and normal activities frozen. It seems remarkably easy for our imagination to stop the mysterious force that we call time. If one stops the processes, then there is nothing to mark time. Is there time when nothing changes anywhere? Even if there was, what would be the point?

It is a fact that the only way that we measure time is by measuring changes. Every single clock in the world is simply a measure of changes. That is all. We count the number of "ticks" in whatever clock we are using, whether it is an old pendulum clock, an atomic clock, digital watch, or the carbon atom (carbon dating), and then declare the time that has passed. I believe most people think that in order to measure changes, time must pass. But what if it were the other way around? What if changes were the driving force that creates the environment that we call time?

The river is a favorite allegory for time. But if you look closely at a river, you will realize that the river is controlled by the water even though it looks the other way around. For example, if you take enough water out of the river, the river will stop. Put too much water in and it will flood. The Grand Canyon is a spectacular example of this. It did not spring into being to guide the water into what is now called the Colorado River. It was movement of the water that dug out the huge canyon.

Time is like the river. Changes are the actions that gouge out the valleys that we call time. Once a valley has been dug by changes, then the changes tend to follow the path it made. But if there are no changes, then there is no time. Our definition of time is simply a convenience for us to group changes together and to anticipate converging events. A converging event is like the sun rising and knowing that it is time to go to work. This convergence is called "Monday" for a lot of people. The Monday is purely a fiction that we made up. There is nothing outside our say so that makes it Monday. If all technology failed and the whole world had amnesia for a decade, what day would it be when we all woke up?

If there were no restrictions to energy, the first time there was an explosion of a big enough magnitude it would tear apart the atomic bonds all over the universe, destroying all life. Nothing would have an opportunity to develop in this environment. Our universe contains certain rather convenient laws that restrict the presence of energy to levels that prevent universal annihilation.

One of these can be seen in light. Nothing with mass can travel faster than the speed of light. If any mass could go at any speed it wanted, we would have the potential for universal destruction, because the faster something goes the greater the force it has when it strikes. Unlimited speed means unlimited power which allows unlimited destruction.

Changes are a measure of power, because nothing can change or cycle without power. Therefore, the universe only allows so many changes within a certain space; otherwise we would be open to universal destruction. When something changes distance from you, it is a change. If something is not moving relative to you but it is on fire, that is also a change. However, there must be a limit to the balance of stationary change to relative distance change. In other words, if you are expressing your maximum change in the form of speed, then no other changes would be allowed. From this, we can conclude that there must be a maximum allowable speed.

It would follow that within this maximum allowable speed, no changes could be observed. And it is so. If you experience something going past you at near the speed of light, "time" will be almost stopped within that object. As Einstein said, changes (time) slows as the relative speed approaches the speed of light.

If there is no relative speeds then one can express a maximum amount of change relative to the mass present according to this equation: $E = MC^2$. Since we know that matter is based on discreet blocks (quanta) we also know that there can be only so much matter present within a certain volume. That is the maximum amount of energy expressible when there is no relative speed.

This also can be seen as everything being limited to the speed of light since all change boils down to movement at some level (what we experience as heat is moving molecules, for example) and all movement can be calculated as relative speed. But that is a little misleading because speed is traditionally calculated by using time, something that is also not definable in absolute terms.

All limits we experience in both time and energy can be expressed as a maximum amount of change allowable relative to any object in the universe. Time is simply not necessary. All energy is expressed in the form of changes. Time is simply a convenience for humankind to foresee when certain changes will come about relative to their own normal internal changes.

So, it is quite possible for humankind to grow, evolve, and die out before some living things in this universe make a single change. If that were the case, we would have no scientific means of even registering their existence. It is fortunate that we have more than science to work with.

Things change at their own rate. For emergent behavior to occur, we need interaction to happen frequently enough that the individual agents carry the effect of one interaction over to the next interaction. If there is no time, then perhaps consciousness and memories exist in entirely different time-scales than those to which we are accustomed. It is possible that this consciousness then could link us up through time as if time had never passed.

For example, someone might be connected to one of these consciousnesses that stretch across our lifetimes and they might sense a personality from hundreds of years ago. We might call this a ghost. Even more interesting is how this kind of consciousness might nest quicker cycling entities within it. There are many possibilities here.

This type of consciousness might also be very good at seeing the outcome of certain actions. For example, people talk about how when it becomes inevitable that an accident is about to happen, time slows right down. Even so, there is nothing they can do to change anything because a series of events has been put into effect that creates an unchangeable outcome.

If the sun exploded right now as you are reading this, it would take at least eight minutes for us even to be able to see it or detect it with any known instrument. Even if someone realized that in eight minutes we would see the sun explode. Still, even if we somehow knew it had exploded there is nothing to be done to save ourselves with only eight minutes left. Not enough changes can take place in eight minutes to create any significant difference to this outcome.

As obvious as this looks, perhaps to a consciousness that spans eons some things that we believe to be impossible to predict are actually inevitable. It is our short lifespan that prevents us from perceiving the larger forces at work. Perhaps this is the original argument for destiny. If someone were to find a way to tap into a consciousness like this it might look like they were a prophet.

However, the ability to predict would be very limited because we do live in a chaotic system that is sensitive to initial conditions. Every single one of you will have a profound effect on society in the future. Whatever you do in your life, however short, will be absorbed by the feedback processes within society and be loudly expressed at some point in the future.

If we keep in mind that time is simply change, perhaps we could call an consciousness that exists throughout the life cycle of the universe a time consciousness.

Though I think that this time consciousness is likely to exist and I can perhaps vaguely describe it, I don't think anyone can actually grasp the whole of it because it lies well outside our conscious ability to fully comprehend.

Past-life regression is an interesting phenomenon. People are regressed and sometimes come up with obscure but verifiable detail from the lifetimes they are remembering, occasionally from hundreds of years ago. Sometimes, this information was unknown until an investigation began. Past life regression rarely takes someone into a famous life, by the way.

Here is another interesting fact. Many people have a deep fear of spiders. This is seen as irrational by many "rational" people. However, if you follow the human evolution back into the mists of the ancient past, you will discover that our direct genetic ancestors (long before we looked human) were the prey of spiders three to four times our size. While spiders take on many shapes and sizes, the horrifying giant spider creations in horror movies almost always take on the form that hunted us so long ago, even in films and television programs made before we knew this.

One way we engage our discontinuous mind is by chopping up life's experiences. The cells in our body live and die continuously while we hold what we call ourselves present. The life that you are expressing right now is part of an unbroken chain of life that stretches back to the first living things on earth. Every single one of you is the result of success after success after success through billions of years. It is your ancestors that defeated the threat of the spiders. It is your ancestors that managed to survive the unbelievably hot, dry, empty deserts of Pangaea. They also managed to survive the millions of years of domination by the dinosaurs. Your ancestors shrugged off meteor strikes, ice ages, plagues, wars and everything reality could throw at them and yet they still raised living children that resulted in you reading this now.

Do you really think we have no mechanism to hold onto lessons from these times? It is not quite like the memory we use day-to-day, but it is a memory. Since it is more important to humankind as a whole than it is to individuals, I imagine that is where it resides. When we tap into the humankind consciousness, we then have access to memories regardless of when they occurred.

As such, those who a stronger connection with these memories remember being stalked with intent by a creature stronger than us, with a killing venom, and that saw us only as food for its life and offspring. When they catch sight of a spider, the part of them that evolved to fear spiders for their own survival suddenly remembers, and for a split second it is as if it were a thousand millions years ago. They scream.

Snakes (their ancestors at least), sharks, and scorpions were also prominent in our past.

There is a flip side to this. If we remember, so will other species. Humankind is destroying life at an incredible rate right now. If you belong to another animal species, unless you are a well-treated human pet, you will likely fear humans more than any other thing on earth. The Native Americans are quoted as saying that the west wasn't wild until the white men came. One of the things they witnessed is how animal behavior dramatically changed once the wholesale slaughter began in North America. For example, bears used to respect man. After the arrival of the Europeans they became dangerous, especially if they had cubs. They began to strike out, just as any powerful creature (or country) does when made afraid. The forests took on a darker aspect. Now one had to tread carefully where before it was simply home.

Today, there are isolated populations of bears that have not experienced the slaughter. They will gently play with you if you approach them correctly and even allow you in their dens. They won't even allow other bears in their dens. This is how all of nature could be for us if we acted differently.

The problem was that some societies saw man as separate from all other life and so ignored all the balance points. Off they went on an incredibly destructive killing spree. We haven't stopped to this day. And if we remember the spiders from millions of years ago, surely these other animals will remember what we are doing to them today. They might not always be as helpless relative to us as they are now. There is a saying I like; be nice to others on your way up so they will be nice to you on your way down. I think we are sowing some very bad seeds that could come back at us with a frightening fury. I think we really need to become much more conscious of what we are doing in the world.

Once you practice looking at the world in a continuous fashion, you eventually come to realize that our intimate connection with the earth can deeply move you. Earth is your home and all the different life forms here really are your brothers and sisters. Even the plants share huge sections of identical DNA with us.

Just like in our human families, we may fight from time to time, but the earth is all we have. Even if we do manage to go to another planet, it will never feel anything like this. We really should take much better care of it than we have done recently.

I think it is highly likely that our consciousness is pretty much immortal. As it moves through time it won't now take on the exact attributes that you have today, but it will always be part of the emergent system that is the human species.

However, this is definitely one area where I think the more belief systems we can link up, the better our understanding will be.

The Back Side of the Power Curve

With all the love and awareness that does exist in humankind our emergent behavior has become the most terrifying monster ever to stride the earth. It destroys habitat, kills off entire species, and vast populations of animals experience torturous deaths at its hands. Just about anything on earth big enough to be noticed by humans is being terrified, modified, or overridden by our emergent behavior. And God help you if you get caught up by some research facilities. This is a direct reflection of how unconscious we are on a global level.

While I respect the desire of vegetarians to stop cruelty to animals, getting upset at the fact that we eat chicken eggs (for example) while munching on seeds, which are the result of a plant's best attempt to reproduce itself, seems no more aware to me than what the meat handlers are doing. There is nothing on earth that has a desire to have its life process stopped so it can be deconstructed in the digestive tract of another species.

To suggest that plants "want" to be eaten looks to me to be a self-serving way to favor one form of life over another because its processes look more like ours. Even fruit doesn't "want" to be eaten; what it wants is for as many of its seeds to find fertile soil in order to grow and thrive. If you eat an orange and throw the seeds in the ground in a cold climate you have destroyed the precious efforts of that plant. Our activity in the plant world has been just as heartless as in the animal world. We have bent many plants to live as we will rather than as they would normally express themselves, while dramatically reducing the presence of wild plants. Life is life, no matter how a discontinuous mind decides to categories things.

But we have to eat to live. Because, unless you are a plant, you can't survive by basking in the sunlight. Your life processes are simply too fast for energy of the sunlight to sustain you.

Humankind is biologically wired to be omnivorous. We ignore the optimum created by millions of years of emergent forces at our own peril. While some people might live quite healthily on an entirely vegetarian diet, that might not be true for everyone. Some Inuit communities in Canada had lived for centuries without ever seeing fruits or vegetables. They also had never seen cancer. Cancer appeared for the first time in their history after modern man flew up fruits and vegetables to enhance the Inuit's normal diet of seal meat and blubber, along with some fish. Must we conclude that everyone must eat blubber and avoid fruit and vegetables in order to cure cancer? (By the way, I'm told that blubber-breath is rather off-putting to mainstream people.)

People who want to dictate what we should do as individuals in such detail are rarely aware of the rich variety present in reality. Just because something works for you and/or your people does not necessarily mean it will work for everyone. This is can be especially true when the numbers participating pass a critical number.

But what can we do about the cruelty being perpetrated by our emergent behavior? We have to eat, don't we?

Just as the consequence of pollution is far removed from most individuals actually making the mess, so is the consequence of our diet removed from the majority doing the eating. The few people who actually kill what the rest of society eats are isolated in their task and their feelings are dulled. Animal after animal passes in front of them to be killed. Even more efficient is the use of machines to do it for us. Then, no one has to stare their victim in the eye. Is there a colder way to die than by a machine which was specifically designed to kill you? Perhaps the only human beings who really understood this horror were the victims murdered on an industrial scale in the 1940s. Perhaps some readers remember that the Nazis manufactured a whole range of household items from the bodies of the Jews. This culture was horribly scarred and is one reason why they find themselves trapped in a position of causing such misery in the Middle East. Their emergent behavior is terrified of ever being in a weaker position to anyone ever again and have armed and trained themselves appropriately.

Nature is being traumatized by us, though we rarely feel it as individuals. Our emergent behavior has disconnected us from the ravenous nature of our society in order to maximize efficiency. Meat, fruit, and vegetables appears on our table. It tastes good. That is all many people want to know. These feelings of apathy stem directly from the emergent system that currently guides us.

In many societies that successfully lived in balance with their surroundings, killing for food was a profound act that had to be done with great care and respect. There is little room for unconscious cruelty in systems like this. I realize this is not going to happen any time soon, but if people had to kill what they ate, or wore, or used for ornaments, it would cure many of the ills our presence has inflicted on the living world around us.

Unfortunately, we have another problem. If you are flying an airplane and you want to slow down while maintaining altitude, you back off the power. This is common sense. However, at a critical point, this reverses; in order to go slower you need more power. This is called the back side of the power curve. In some airplanes, it is possible to be flying very slowly at full power, and unable to make any change without losing altitude. You can't slow down, speed up, or turn. At this point the only certainty is that you will be going down. If you started with enough altitude, you can point the airplane towards the ground, speed up and then regain control of your situation. However, if you are too close to the ground, you will crash.

The peak of human society is getting lower and lower. I think there are still some moves we could make that could get us over to the other side of the power curve without a crash, but we are running out of time.

There are a number of aspects of human society where we are now on the back side of our power curve and approaching the point of no return. Food is one of these areas. In the past, it was possible for anyone who wanted to, to head off into the wilderness and live off the land. Nature provided everything needed and asked for nothing in return. The free life was available to anyone who wanted it.

While there are a limited number of places where this can still be done, for the vast majority this is no longer a possibility. You have to work in order to make money in order to have the basics of life. And instead of the three to five hours a day that traditional "primitive" people had to work, we have to work closer to eight, plus all the domestic work that is not normally counted when statistics come out. We are pedaling faster and faster just to maintain altitude. We are on the back side of the standard of living power curve.

Humanity now consumes such a massive amount of food that our system has become dependent on high technology just to keep us fed. This is an incredibly dangerous situation because if at any point we lose significant capacity, mass starvation will result. High technology simply does not have the pedigree of wisdom contained within nature's emergent system. We have some serious weaknesses developing in our commanded food system. For example, mad cow disease, bird flu, and foot and mouth disease were all created because of artificial conditions we forced on our food animals. I suspect that two of these diseases would never have appeared if our animals were not living in overcrowded conditions, and one of the diseases appeared because we fed ground-up cow to cows!

How out of balance do we have to get before we notice the danger? Today, they are still feeding ground-up animal matter to cows in a government approved safe way.

Some very intelligent and educated people who know a lot more about the meat industry than I do were involved in decisions that led up to this behavior. The food industry was simply doing what we command of it; bringing food to the table as cheaply as possible while protecting the consumer from any of the blood or gore involved. This is our emergent behavior in action. This is why it is so important that we make an effort to understand what is happening here.

Similar problems have been occurring in the fruit and vegetable sector as well. Apparently, this is another area where some people think they have the ability to command a better solution into being. The principle of organic farming is sustainable, but unfortunately, we are too far on the back side of the power curve to have organic farming replace the factory farming that currently sustains us. As more of our wild food stocks collapse from over harvesting, we will lean ever more on technology, including genetic engineering. This is why I suggested earlier that our current direction is taking us to a starvation event for humankind.

This blind drive for efficiency is also a problem. In systems, slack is necessary in order to absorb any shocks that life tends to occasionally throw our way. Efficiency takes up the slack. The less slack there is, the less room there is for maneuvering if something goes wrong. If by some unlucky chance our food system (or any system we rely on for that matter) finds a way to take up all the slack in the system (become nearly 100% efficient), the result will be a brittle system working a full power just to maintain altitude. What do you think will happen next?

Technology cannot replace nature because it is a commanded system trying to replace an emergent system. Those who wait in hope of a pill to replace all our nutrition requirements are unlikely to be fulfilled. Even if it did work, we might find our citizenship to earth withdrawn.

The H G Wells novel *War of the Worlds* depicts a vastly superior and immensely strong alien species setting up shop on earth to farm humans for food. Everything man could throw at them was completely ineffective. In the end, they are killed off by the bacteria and viruses present all over the earth. Our place on earth is secured only as long as we remain in partnership with the emergent system that is Gaia. If we take ourselves too far away from earth's natural system, either through isolation or technology, we will become extremely vulnerable to the living emergent system of earth. There is nothing known to man, not even nuclear weapons, capable of killing off all the bacteria and viruses present, and we need them in our bodies to live. These friendly bacteria are perfectly capable of mutating into something less beneficial. There are several diseases, some of them fatal, which are only slightly different versions of bacteria we rely upon to live. (E-coli comes to mind.)

The technological route, if not followed with consciousness, will lead us to the back side of the power curve on many fronts. Our detachment opens the door for a lethal crisis to arrive without warning. In this unconscious state, all of humanity is incredibly vulnerable.

On the other hand, if we work with the natural emergent patterns around us we could create an incredibly joyful, expansive and exciting life for all humankind.

Which world would you rather leave to our children?

Death and Immortality

People frequently talk about living forever without really considering what they are saying. For example, are they suggesting that they want all the cells in their body to live forever? That is impossible because how would you have skin (the surface is dead so you don't bleed to death or dry out in the air), fingernails and hair if none of your cells died? How would your immune system work?

If you want to 'live forever' in the same way as you do now, that means everything in your body must live and die as you dictate. What would you do with a cell that wants to live forever? A cell that has escaped the restrictions of our body's dictated DNA instruction and begun reproducing based on its own local instruction is called cancer. If you believe in free will of everything, then by what moral right do we kill them?

Notice that if we allow the cancerous cells the right to free will they will likely kill the body that keeps them alive, and thus their actions are unknowingly suicidal. What about the free will of the surrounding cells that do not want to die? It gets complicated very quickly. I wonder if the universal consciousness would give the same room to an eternal human that we give to cancer cells?

Just as skin cells must die in order for you to have skin, your body must die for the human race to continue as it has. If you lived forever, you would be stepping out of the human stream of life that has been living and dying for hundreds of thousands of years to successfully bring about you. Not only that, but all the earth uses death as a way to ensure eternal life. You would no longer be part of the stream of life on earth that has been here for billions of years. It is possible that you would no longer be part of the stream of life that is the universe. In fact, I must wonder how the universe would view a body that did not die.

However, if that is what you really want to live forever, then here is how to do it.

Science tells us that the reason we age is that the power units of individual cells leak destructive by-products that then damage surrounding cells. The rate of leakage is directly linked to the way you age. Scientists have been experimenting with this and have managed to use this technology to expand the lifetime of a worm to four times its normal span.

Right now, there are scientists working to do the same with human beings. They predict they can get humans to live to around 1,000 to 1,500 years within the next century, with a quality of life similar to someone in middle age.

Obviously, they are onto something important, and perhaps I will eat my words, but I think they will fail to extend human life to over a thousand years. Here is why.

First of all you need to fully comprehend emergent behavior and how it applies to living bodies, and then it will become obvious that the human body is designed to die. One way you can tell is the way certain parts are non-renewable, such as teeth. Animals that really need strong teeth their entire lives are constantly either growing the same teeth, like mice, or constantly make new teeth, like sharks. Teeth are not designed to be put in the mouth and last forever any more than a single breath is meant to last forever.

Human beings make one adult set and then that's it. If you were designed to live longer, you would have been designed in a different way. This is only one example of many.

To be truly immortal, you will have to change the emergent patterns within your body in order to create constant renewing processes in all the different areas that are currently wearing. Also, you will have to slow everything down.

Death allows human beings to live their whole life at a sprint. If you want to travel twenty miles on foot, you cannot sprint the whole way. Many people cannot even walk the whole way without stopping. What you need to do is set a pace that will manage your resources most efficiently to travel the twenty miles in a reasonable time. If you were to be immortal, you would have to look at the way you live life in a totally different way. Forever is a very long way to travel and getting the energy expenditures right to do this would require great awareness. Sprinting would only be allowed in brief intervals.

Still, you decide you want to live forever and have taken the time to fully understand emergent behavior, and you understand how to create a system within the body that is sustainable forever. Now all you have to do is implement it.

The only way to do that is to create an internal system change. Your whole life would have to slow down considerably. Trees, for example, can live thousands of years, but they don't move around a lot. You also have to decide what to do with all the non-renewable parts of yourself. Some parts, like teeth, can be allowed to drop out permanently, but others are a bit trickier. Your nervous system is non-renewable. That is why if you break your back, you can be paralyzed for life.

Now, some people might claim we will be able to repair all this, especially in the future, but I'm afraid that technology will not be the final answer in the quest for immortality. While a specific injury will eventually be tamed by research, theory of chaos shows us how a lot of tiny malfunctions will eventually cascade into an unstoppable avalanche of problems.

The way to combat this is to make everything in your body totally renewable. We will have to rewire you because there are lots of places that cannot be reached to be repaired naturally. A flippant example is a split end on your hair. The end of your hair is far away from any blood supply or any other living cells. Do you see the problem? There are many parts inside and outside that are simply inaccessible to your body's repair mechanisms. While a split end might not be crucial to your survival, there are many things in your body that are.

Even though I do think it might be possible to be immortal you would no longer be human. Characteristics are the result of the emergent behavior of your entire body. If you change that body too much you will no longer be you. So you would have an immortal shell, but I'm afraid the part of your consciousness that you feel is yourself would be considerably altered.

If you understand emergent behavior and look at the entity called the human race, you will understand that just like skin cells, for humanity to continue in a recognizable form, we have to die. This is what enables us to have so much energy, to combat constantly evolving disease, adjust to changes in our environment, and many other things.

Emergent behavior has the ability to create such high order solutions that they are beyond our understanding. We are the result of emergent behavior taking in all the factors in the entire world and creating the best people it could. People trying to command a better design into existence might first try to design a computer that doesn't crash. A computer is far less complicated than a human being.

Science's inability to comprehend the complexity of emergent systems is demonstrated repeatedly almost every time biologists introduce a new species into an ecosystem in order to fix what they perceive is a problem. There are many stories of disaster here, some of which are today using up fortunes in desperate attempts to avoid the resulting ecological disasters. If we can't improve upon computers and ecosystems, why are we suddenly so certain about genetics in a general sense, and redesigning the human body to live forever in particular? Genetics is a vastly more complicated emergent system than anything we have dealt with before. We have failed spectacularly in trying to improve much simpler systems. I am very skeptical about any sudden improvements in our wisdom in these areas, especially since we have yet to tackle our own emergent behavior.

Genetic engineering of all kinds looks to me like a disaster waiting to happen. If we were only working in the short-term I think the assurances of the scientists would be valid. However, we simply don't understand the long-term implications that will be expressed after tinkering in such a complex emergent systems as the DNA that governs of all the life in the world.

Another concern with eternal life is something Richard Dawkins called bottle-necking. If our body is really built up of different levels of independent living things, then if they were left alone for enough generations then what would prevent them from beginning to evolve in their own right? How would our body cope as more and more sections of it began to carve out their own destinies?

Not well. Tumors and cancers are indications of this beginning to happen.

In order for evolution to occur, mutations must be allowed. Even number sorting computer programs will effectively evolve only if some randomness (mutation) is introduced as the programs reproduce. It is a delicate balance between tumors (too much mutation) and no mutation (vulnerable to disease and other changing environmental factors) that evolution must continually navigate. Who in the world is aware enough of all the factors to better the balance created by the emergent behavior of all of nature?

One of the longest living complex animals in the world is the tortoise. Their cells have a remarkable resistance to mutation, so they don't "age" or die for quite a long time. However, there are two important aspects to this. One is that tortoises have found a successful form that they have not really changed for several million years. They have not stopped evolving, but they are certainly not on the cutting edge. Second, even they die after one or two hundred years.

Like rebooting a computer after a crash, every complex living being on earth uses a reset process to start afresh. If you never reboot a modern computer, it runs slower and slower until it eventually locks up.

The reset button for complex life is the death of individual organism, while the life continuum remains immortal and intact through the thread of reproduction. This enables complex beings to be rebuilt from scratch. Any evolutionary processes can easily be incorporated.

As Dawkins points out, can you imagine how difficult it would be for evolution to implement an improvement to a heart that can never stop beating? It would have to tear down all the cells while maintaining the old integrity while rebuilding the new design. You would become quite vulnerable while all this was going on. If you want to live forever then you will need to accommodate this going on in different parts of your body for the rest of eternity.

Without death as a survival mechanism you would likely be unable to withstand the presence of any disease. Because we die anyway, death by disease is just one more step in the overall dance of life. The surviving elements of your race carry exactly what is needed to keep surviving.

This is how disease can adjust so quickly to antibiotics. It is every species' survival mechanism. Eternal life would instantly render this ubiquitous survival mechanism powerless.

If you live forever, your immune system will slowly become out of date and useless, just like an antivirus program on your computer that has not been updated. Pathogens would become increasingly lethal to you. Keeping you in a sterilized situation would be a monumental technical challenge. For example, how would you deal with bacteria that evolved to become pathogens from the stock of cooperative bacteria in your body? Just because you decide to stop using death as a powerful evolutionary tool doesn't mean the bacteria in your body will do the same.

I would rather trust the emergent pattern that has sustained us for millions of years rather than some human commanded modification trying to make us live forever. In fact, I am almost certain that if someone actually succeeded, the result would have devastating consequences in some unforeseen way.

For an individual, ageing and death sucks. But it only takes a few seconds of contemplation before its wisdom is evident. The scientist that is trying to extend life to 1000 years said his goal was to stop the 100,000 deaths that occur due to natural causes every year in the UK alone. Where would we put all these extra people? Does that mean we would have to stop having children? Are only new generations allowed to have children or are all the generations allowed children? If we all live to a thousand years old and we all breed we will have an explosion of humanity. To the earth, it might even look like a cancer.

While it might be fascinating for some to view life from the point-of-view of being an unevolving human among the young and constantly improving human variations, I am not interested in living that way.

If everyone came to understand emergent behavior, older people could once again be valued for their growing understanding of the patterns around us. Then perhaps we would stop the desperate fight to prevent ourselves from appearing wise.

The people in cultures that embraced emergent behavior rarely feared death. Everything conspired towards understanding and contentment rather than fear and resentment. How much angst could excise from our society if we weren't peddling so hard to avoid what the life systems of earth has found to be best possible outcome?

As things stand, many health systems in the wealthy countries cannot spend enough money to keep up. Budget constraints continually cause people to die who did not have to die that day. Some people are outraged at this apparent coldness while others moan at the ever increasing tax levels needed to support the health care system. But these decisions will until we divert every single penny we have into health care. Even then, someone is going to have to decide who should live and who should die. What an extraordinary burden that society is demanding of it health care system, and the economy in general.

Just because we can spend enormous fortunes in extending life does not necessarily mean we should.

I know the lure of eternal life. I lived with that possibility for years. Even though some part of me still insists it might be possible, I have to notice that there is not one single human being living on earth living today is significantly older than a normal human lifetime. If it is possible, then the ability will have to come from something we have never tapped into in all the history of people since the beginning of life. It would also have to be wise enough to deal with all the problems of emergent behavior that are mentioned here (and more) before it will be viable. We will know if anyone succeeded because the evidence of a successful eternal life is eternal, isn't it?

It won't be genetic manipulation that succeeds because if there was any advantage to living forever, nature would have worked that out eons ago, as it did for some yeast. But keep in mind, nature has designed everything around the yeast so that a non-ageing life emerged. It did not do this for us or for any other complex animal on earth.

Perhaps immortality is only something we can look forward to if we become a greater participant in some the larger life-giving emergent systems that may be present in our universe.

Expressing It All

In science, chaos shows us how even the tiniest inputs will, over time, completely change the position of a system. If you hold your breath right now, you will possibly change a hot day into a cold one a hundred years hence. Some of these tiny inputs can be the trigger for massive events. So how are we positioned to notice these inputs?

Our brains do not hear sound directly; we have hairs in our ears that interpret the vibrations in the air. That information is sent to our brains via nerves. Our brain then tells us, based on previous experience and conditioning, what those vibrations should sound like. The information goes through numerous systems in our bodies before we become aware of the sound. Our brains never hear the sound directly.

We never see light directly, either. As George Stratton famously demonstrated in 1896, if you constantly wear glasses that turn the world upside down, after a few days the brain makes an adjustment to what it thinks should be out there and the world turns right side up again. But if you then take the glasses off the world will appear upside down to your naked eye. If your brain can so easily match the physical reality of seeing to how you think things should be seen, then how hard do you think it would be for your beliefs to alter your perception of reality in any way it wants?

This whole process can be intercepted at any time. The concept behind the movie *The Matrix* was that computers directly accessed different points in our perception networks and sent signals along our nervous system that would naturally be there if we were actually in that situation. As *The Matrix* also pointed out, how your brain interprets these signals can completely change your experience, regardless of what the reality really is.

Many believe that children are better able to see the unexpected than adults. The younger the child the more they see and the less they are "judgmental". A child learning to read handwriting has trouble discerning letters because everything is new. The 'i' you just wrote is a little different from the first one you wrote and the child immediately sees that. The child points at the second 'i' and asks, "What is that?"

You patiently explain. "It's an 'i'."

The child correctly learns that written 'i's are not precise but fall within certain parameters and then unconsciously factors out the true variations. The reality that every written 'i' is different fades to the background. The blanks will be filled in and extraneous protrusions filtered out so that anything that looks vaguely like an 'i' will automatically be admitted to their brain so that they see the 'i'. The child now recognizes an 'i' for an 'i'.

All through their childhood we teach children how to organize the infinite information that they will meet in reality. However, each lesson learned erodes their ability to perceive what is actually there. This is why young children are so good at seeing things that adults frequently miss. Their filters are not fully in place yet.

However, we must develop filters because our ability to take in information is finite. By learning to discard certain information we can then open ourselves up to other kinds of information. The final pattern of information acceptance and rejection resulting from this process is a powerful component that makes up your unique identity.

There are many different ways to organize the information, all of which have their strengths and weaknesses. Among the most powerful tools to organize information is a belief system.

One of the main purposes of belief systems is to illuminate the important aspects of the world. For example, if you believe that owls are a sign of death, then the appearance of an owl is extremely important. For those who believe that someone who can heal a disease with a plant is aligned with the devil, then the presence of a herbal practice becomes impossible to ignore. For others who believe that only medical doctors can heal, the presence of a herbalist is completely irrelevant.

There is so much reality in the world, that different belief systems can create a completely different experience for those holding them. Is it any wonder that we sometimes battle over what is "reality"?

Of course, all of this filtering of reality is bound to create blank spots. Since we know that the tiniest details can become system-wide triggers, if we only relied on our minds we would be in trouble. Fortunately, there is another tool we have evolved.

What is the weather like today? Well, technically there is an infinite amount of data, but it can all be summed up in a quick sentence. It is "cold" today. That is all most people need to know in order to have a relevant understanding of the state of the weather. If you were to describe to them all the temperatures over the world, all the winds and highs and lows, the simple understanding they are looking for might become lost in accurate detail.

The world effectively has an infinite amount going on at any given time and an incomprehensible number of ways to interact with a human being. Anywhere in there could be a crucial system-changing piece of information. How can you possibly remain alert to it?

It's easy. You ask someone how they feel.

A healthy emotional body is amazingly sensitive to the state of its surroundings. Someone is about to board an airplane and suddenly feels a deep foreboding. They don't board. The airplane crashes. How often have we heard that?

After all we have discussed, do you think it is impossible for the emotions to have picked up something from somewhere, even perhaps from a consciousness that we aren't aware of ourselves, and given a warning?

The presence of emotions is an extraordinary survival tool. Not one single free animal died in the Asian tsunami. Rats flee sinking ships. How do they know not to keep seeking air pockets? Something tells them that their best chance for survival is to jump into the ocean long before a ship actually sinks. I doubt it is their intellect.

Emotions are a vital key to survival because they fill in the gap in awareness that our minds are ill suited to tackle. The caveat here is that the emotions must be healthy. Transferring old feelings onto new situations is not being aware. Every situation is different even if they look alike. People who have buried their emotions will keep getting signals about situations and events that are long past that are unlikely to have relevance in the moment. Healthy emotions pick up all the crucial details in the relevant moment and will send a single emotional message. That emotion is a state that contains all the details of the situation, including the ones overlooked by our filtering minds.

Emotions are another example of how emergent behavior has created something far beyond the parts making it up. It is also why it is so hard for our mind to fully understand. However, it can be a magical tool to those who work to develop it to its full potential.

On the other hand, it is possible for people to use reality filters to blunt the sensitivity of both the mind and the emotions so that they walk their entire life in a fog of their own making. Frequently, these people construct powerful perceptions and arguments to keep them safe from anyone not holding the similar reality filters. Their filters become a force of disconnection in the world.

I call this manifestation the belief box.

The Belief Box

Most people are far better experts of their own beliefs than anyone approaching from the outside. Seeing off challenges is a simple and natural reflex to any mature belief. If you want to experience mind-boggling mental agility, try to trap someone in a contradiction of their belief. I guarantee, the only people that will give way are those who are already looking for a way out.

But sometimes the belief's defense becomes so strong that what began as a means to organize reality becomes a system to redefine reality. As with statistics, there is so much information in reality that people can pick and choose a set of facts that will prove just about anything they want it to prove. This allows us to create pretty much any reality we want to in our minds.

This filtering begins the process of disconnecting the belief from the reality around it. When this happens, the belief no longer evolves with the rest of human understanding and it begins to need stronger and stronger filters to protect it from contradictory information. Eventually, the belief becomes boxed and locked away from general access. It ends up like a museum piece instead of part of the living breathing world outside.

People protecting boxed beliefs are frequently very fervent and have a propensity for radical thoughts and deeds. But before we judge, it is important to understand just how easy it is to box our beliefs.

As we saw, perception is a tricky thing. Like the child learning to read an "i", we learn how to filter reality to distinguish what is important. However, routinely discarding significant parts of reality leaves us very susceptible to deceiving ourselves about reality.

Even people trained to see totally objectively can be fooled by their own filters. For centuries, scientists were trained by the best schools in rigorous methods of factoring out "noise" in their experiments. This "noise" turned out be a crucial part of reality that scientist now acknowledge with what has been popularly dubbed as chaos theory.

How significant was this new reality?

Because chaotic behavior turned out to be described by non-linear equations, it started to be called non-linear science. In James Gleick's book, *Chaos*, Stanislaw Ulam is quoted as saying "that to call the study of chaos 'nonlinear science' was like calling zoology 'the study of nonelephant animals'." The scope of what scientists were trained not to see was extraordinary.

It was puzzling for some how society's most rigidly trained investigative minds could miss something so obvious for hundreds of years. To demonstrate how human minds respond to the unexpected, James Gleick describes an experiment in *Chaos*.

In the 1940's, a pair of psychologists were conducting an experiment on volunteers. The people were briefly shown a playing card and were asked to call out what they saw. For example, if they saw the ten of hearts, they called out ten of hearts. Could anything be simpler?

Of course, there was a catch. Some of the cards were changed into something that normally does not exist. For example, a queen of spades were turned red instead of black, or the ace of diamonds might be turned black. When these freakish cards were shown only briefly, the subjects had no problem calling out an answer. It was wrong, of course. When shown a red six of spades, they would simply call out "six of hearts" or "six of spades". But nothing here upset their world view.

However, when shown the cards more slowly, their filters were challenged. They hesitated. They were aware there was a problem but couldn't identify it. The subjects would say they saw something odd, like a red border around a black heart. Do you see how the filters were changing what people are actually seeing?

Eventually, they slowed down the pace enough that most people caught on. Once they made the mental shift to their filter, everything was fine. However, not everyone was able to do this. A few people clung to their reality filter. They suffered a sense of disorientation that brought on real pain. Even allowed to stare at the cards they said things like "I can't make that suit out, whatever it is," or "It didn't even look like a card that time. I don't know what color it is now or whether it's a spade or heart. I'm not even sure what a spade looks like. My God!"

This is how powerful filters can be. If a person is experiencing the world from a belief box guarded by filters this powerful, there is no way that I am aware of to reach them. Trying to force a way through the filters can cause real pain and trauma. It is important not to underestimate the power of a belief box on others or yourself.

Even in the simplistic reality of playing cards, where the solution could be found within only eight possibilities, there were a few who could not find a solution to their reality filter that insisted spades were always black. They fought hard to keep their little truth even though contrary proof stood right before their eyes. What chance does someone have when the possibilities are endless as in all of reality? If a person's mindset is wired to refuse certain information, that information will not be received, no matter how "obvious" anyone else thinks it is.

In 2002, in England, a seventeen-year-old man killed an old woman, cut out her heart and drank her blood during a rigorously observed procedure to turn himself into a vampire. This was his belief. I know for a fact that his belief was not reality because he did not, after all, turn into a vampire the way he wanted.

Can you put yourself inside this person's belief box? His truth was that vampires existed and they lived forever, which was one of his stated motivations for wanting to be a vampire. He planned to live near a lot of old people that others would not miss. It would be a great place for a vampire to live, he said. His belief box was obvious and deadly.

Now, for all those who do not believe in vampires, this looks to be an absurd situation. But this is just an example of what can happen to anyone's picture of reality if they consistently practice factoring out reality where it conflicts with their boxed belief. We all do it to a certain extent.

It is not really important what your belief is, as long as you allow it room to evolve as reality is presented to you. Beliefs and filters are not problems unless they are held rigidly with the purposes of trying forcing all of reality to reside in one belief. Then, anyone living in a part of reality outside of that prescribed belief will need to be dealt with, one way or another. Dangerous disconnections take place when this happens.

Where people group themselves around a belief, a group belief box can occur. In this case, filters can combine with the power of emergent behavior and the boxed belief can become a power in its own right. These beliefs rise up and take on the qualities of a living entity within society. When this happens, instead of beliefs serving people, people frequently end up serving beliefs.

Absolutely anything can reside inside a belief box and it will all completely logical and reasonable to those inside. Do you want to be a success, an enlightened soul, an objective person, a holy person, a returning spirit, a martyred hero, or simply right? A belief box can instantly put you there with nary a finger lifted.

The seduction of this process cannot be overstated. Any dream we wish can be effortlessly achieved within a well-defended belief box. The problem is the dream is not rooted in reality and reality will continually pressure the belief. If the belief box has to keep out a lot of reality, the pressure from reality will be great and the belief box will feel the need to defend itself. Keep in mind, that almost the United States' massive nuclear and chemical and biological arsenal is considered a defense. A defensive posture of an individual, group, or country, regardless of whether it is rooted in reality or not, can create a very real danger in the world.

Even if the person in the belief box lives and dies in blissful ignorance, the people will be affected. Normally, these people are constantly searching for ways to trap others in the same belief box. Even if they don't succeed, it creates a subtle disconnection field all around them. It within these disconnections that some of society's darker deeds are nurtured.

People will defend a boxed belief using any and all means in their possession. Any threat, including reality, will be attacked with vigor. It will be just a matter of time before the pressure inside someone's belief box creates enough heat that something will boil over. If the belief is experiencing real oppression the response can be very intense indeed.

Keeping our belief's filters soft and malleable is very important for a healthy society. Suggesting that we have a look outside our beliefs is not a suggestion that a belief is invalid, any more than pulling a drowning person from water is an act invalidating the need for water. It is the recognition of the need for air.

While a belief is a wonderful home for our consciousness, we do need to get out sometimes. Otherwise, we can become locked away from the full potential of reality, trapped inside a box of our own making, drowning with our beliefs without realizing what is happening.

Some of those who detect the trap of other peoples' belief boxes move to "rescue" those drowning inside. Unfortunately, intended rescuers can easily find themselves being attacked by those they sought to rescue, especially if the rescuer seeks to drag people out of their belief boxes only to drown them in another.

One characteristic that is common among these rescuers is they are experts at Being Right.

There was a period where I was an accomplished practitioner in the dark art of Being Right. If we were in conversation, I could easily find flaws in your arguments. I would lock onto the problem, pull in the realities you omitted, and skillfully take apart your arguments. Even if I could not convince you of my "rightness" at least I knew what you said was not relevant to me. This neatly safeguarded my belief system and gave me a feeling of superiority. My ability to cut your ideas down proved it.

It also ensured that new information or experience was very difficult for me to access since I knew it all already. It took me a long time to become aware that my biggest barrier to greater understanding was my ability to be right all the time.

Fortunately, a part of me rose up and nudged me to see what would happen if I applied my own unassailable techniques to my own beliefs. With a sense of bemusement, I found that the arguments supporting my beliefs fell just as quickly.

Obviously, if I wanted to achieve the level of open-mindedness to which I aspired, I would have to drop the armor of Being Right. The change was quite dramatic. From all ideas and experiences presented to me, I began to search for little nuggets of truth instead of how I could go on Being Right. My treasure chest bulged. Suddenly life was a fascinating tapestry of new understandings and experiences as I sought how people were right instead of how they were wrong.

At the time, I had thought I had finally reached my goal of being fully open-minded. It was some years before I recognized yet another key reality filter. The following (with some embellishments) actually occurred while I was trying to think of an effective way to explain emotional filters.

"OUCH!!"

The fan casing above the stove just hit my head! My rage takes over. Whack! I hit the stupid fan back. Bloody thing hurting my head like that. It's lucky I didn't rip the evil thing from the wall and hurl it into oblivion.

I growl and swear, expressing the part of me that wants to annihilate the fan.

All done. Except for my aching head I feel all right. I don't use my head that often anyway. The fan remains unbroken, functional and apparently unmoving, cunningly waiting for its next chance to leap out and rap my head. And you just wait to see what I do if it dares…

Led by an unconscious emotional assumption, these short moments contain the entire life cycle of a little truth, a truth created by belief filters that is actually not part of reality. It does not easily shift when confronted by reality or facts, and therefore can create a powerful wall to a person's ability to see the larger truth around them.

I feel my emotions very strongly. When I hit my head I am flooded with powerful feelings that need resolution. In order for feelings to evolve they need to be validated. It is natural for people to try to validate feelings by painting reality in a way that means their emotions are literally right. In this instance, because I felt like a victim, then the fan must have attacked me. My need to be emotionally right created the filter that then blocked out reality.

In order to find suitable environment for this little truth to live and breathe, I began to disconnect for reality. I forced my belief into a shielded box that only allowed officially sanction filtered reality into it. My filters are primed to fend off any facts sent by reality that could prove me wrong. My stance has become: "Come on, world, I'm ready for you!"

This is all unconscious, of course.

Consciously I know the fan attacked. I have to defend myself! This little truth I have created is very seductive because it means that my hitting my head is not my fault. But this new boxed reality creates new needs and desires. If the fan hit me, it means I am not safe until the fan knows that I am far more dangerous than it is. In order to accomplish this, I take on a defensive stance and prepare my defensive response.

Whack!

I hit the fan back. Luckily I have retained enough consciousness to know not to hit it as hard as I would like to emotionally. Otherwise, I will have to fix it. Since this understanding does not in any way conflict with my little truth that the fan attacked me, she remains comfortably nestled in my arms.

I cuss and swear and the emotional charge diminishes. My belief struggles in her box. Her voice is faint over the noise of my emotions. "Are you sure of your facts here?"

My little truth mistress squirms uncomfortably in my arms, but I comfort her. It is a stupid question. Of course I know my facts.

Don't I?

Being ever vigilant, it dawns on me that there is a possibility that the fan might have never left the wall. Even if, in its evil metallic heart, it wanted to hit me, there is no means of locomotion that I am aware of for it to do so. If this is true, then it is actually more likely that I, in fact, hit the fan. Twice. Once with my head and once with my hand. Emotionally, I don't like this, but it is the truth.

My mistress shakes her head emphatically. "No! You were the victim. Somehow, you were attacked, we just have to find out how."

Hmmm. Maybe I should prepare a pre-emptive strike.

But something squirms inside of me. I study my seductive little truth. "It feels good to believe this, but I worry about my relationship with reality."

She starts pouting. "Don't I make you feel good? Can't we just be alone together?"

I smile softly. "You do feel good. But being with you somehow makes me feel somehow disconnected from the rest of the world. Sometimes, it even makes me feel like the world is against me. I have heard that two is the loneliest number since the number one. I really want a healthy relationship with reality as well."

She pouts. Even diminished, the emotions make the relationship look very enticing. Shaking my head at myself, I gather my willpower and dump this flirtatious little truth.

Now it seems obvious that the fan did not hit me.

My belief climbs out of the box I put her in and takes a deep breath. She looks pointedly at me. "It is not the fan's fault. It is your fault," she observes.

Poor fan.

My belief rolls her eyes but takes my hand anyway. I'm embarrassed for being so easily fooled. Fortunately, my belief understands these little affairs. She knows, now, that I will never take these little truths to heart and keep her in a box. Even so, I am working hard to end even these short affairs. They can be so destructive!

This is a very simple example, but it takes only a moment to find other examples of emotions and the resulting seductive little truths that are impossible to put to the reality test, especially when dealing with people. Are you so certain that they meant to hurt you? Did they in fact hurt you, or did you hurt yourself and then unconsciously blame them? There are even a few people that would believe that the fan did indeed jump out and hit me.

As impossible as this may sound, some would even believe that I deserved it.

While beliefs are an important part of us, if they are locked away from everything that might challenge them, then they simply become a trap for our consciousness. Connections at all levels are crucial if we are to bring the experience into the world that many people say they want.

Saying your belief is the only right one and nothing in reality can change it means it is not connected. This is your choice, but I would like to point out that life is change and when all change stops in a living being, the result is frequently death.

On the other hand, a breathing evolving belief that is constantly optimizing its relationship with reality can be a treasure shared by us all. The beautiful delicate dance of our beliefs and reality can help us, heal us, and color our world with vivid, breathtaking, life-giving pictures. Where our beliefs are boxed from reality, they curl onto themselves, darkening, struggling, seeking sustenance to replace the nurturing that reality would have given them, and if we force our boxed beliefs on others we can commit our most heinous acts.

The Emergence of Love

I don't think it is possible for me alone to be fully aware of what I'm about to try to describe. I really need more people with more beliefs to help get a sense of the entire picture. However, for the sake of completeness, I am going to give this my best shot.

Reality is laced with life at all levels in an interlocking dance from the dawn of time. There are different consciousnesses and possibilities throughout the universe. They are all entities in their own right, with their own destinies and unique ways of expressing themselves.

All these agents will create their own emergent forces. There will be enough distinctly separate emergent patterns that they could act as agents in their own right to create another layer of emergent behavior. Different self-aware consciousnesses can form at several different points within these layers. As many layers of this as there are, somewhere in our universe, there will be one that is the highest and most aware consciousness that exists.

Some claim that humans hold this position. In order for humans to be aware, we need our cells to cooperate over our entire lifetime, creating a stable platform from which our consciousness operates. When that order breaks down, our life fails. From our experience, let us assume that any self-aware consciousness requires some sort of stability or order, even if might be unrecognizable to us at certain levels.

But what if people are not, in fact, the pinnacle of awareness in the universe. What if something like that described in the Continuous Consciousness chapter does exist? In order for any universal consciousness to maintain itself, it would need some way to create and hold present a universal integrity. So, what is the glue that can create integrity and meaning from everything, everywhere and everywhen?

A universal consciousness would be the top self-aware layer of emergent behavior made up of other emergent systems. If this is the case, it would possess a consciousness control of all the powers of emergent behavior plus the ability to make moment by moment changes to key control places such as nodal points, critical points and the usually invisible tiny inputs that are destined to become crucial system changers over time. It would have also access to all the different time scales, meaning that it would likely be equally aware of a human lifetime, earth's lifetime, or a quark.

Some might wonder why I assume a universal consciousness wants life at all. Most reasons are impossible to articulate, but I can suggest that if it did not want life everything in the universe would have been extinguished long ago. Not only is it seeking life, but it is likely striving for the highest possible state of all aspects of life.

In order to reach the highest state possible, this consciousness would require an irresistible force that brings about an enthusiastic cooperation between an infinite number of disparate parts. Otherwise, it is unlikely to be able to survive any more than we can if we have tumors and cancers running through our bodies. If different parts are fighting one another to destruction, the larger consciousness will lose health, or integrity, until it reaches the point that the entire emergent system collapses. It will die.

Obviously, the best tool to bring together everything in integrity no matter where it began is emergent behavior. But the health of the whole universe would be riding on its design, so this one would have to be a cracker. Even if it is there, is there any way that we, as tiny little elements within whole universe, could possibly touch or sense this system?

Remember how I mentioned that emotions have an extraordinary ability to sum up huge complex states in a single feeling? It is one of our most powerful tools to connect with things far greater than ourselves. In fact, it might be one of our links to everything.

In order to discuss love I should first properly define it, but I don't think I can. It is a different experience to different people.

Science has some interesting things to say about love. Apparently, the chemical make-up in our brains when we fall romantically in love mirrors those of certain mental illnesses. Reality becomes slightly skewed and our judgment is impaired. Certain chemicals, like serotonin, flood our system making us feel euphoric. But after about five years, no matter how good the initial relationship, the chemicals go back to normal levels. The swept-off-our-feet feeling ends. Many relationships can fall apart at this point.

The article describing this went on to explain how evolution developed this to create the ideal environment to successfully bring up a child. But the first thing I wonder is why would something like this evolve? Again, why not a simple compulsion to have sex (already present for many) and then a similar compulsion to protect any resulting child?

From what I understand of nature and biology, love is not needed to survive. If nature had evolved purely on a need to procreate, a compulsion to protect your offspring would work just as well, the same way we need to breathe air. Few are in love with breathing, but somehow we just keep on doing it anyway regardless of other desires. Try to stop breathing right now if you want to experience how effective compulsions are. In evolutionary terms, love is not needed.

On the other hand, how would it perform as the glue for a universal consciousness?

Universal love could be a consciousness in its own right made up at least partly by us and is almost certainly beyond our ability to comprehend. If love is the glue and guide to all creation, then getting to know love would be the best way to harness the power of creation in your favor.

To access this emergent system, I think it is important to open our beliefs and feelings to reality. We can't love something when we have judgments and unconsidered feelings about the world around us because then we are not properly connected. Love is best experienced when well connected.

Love means different things to different people, and we must be careful not to judge. Please excuse me while I engage my discontinuous mind in order to create some examples.

Is killing wrong? Predators do it all the time. Are they unloving?

Some are. Orcas that have decided to eat the tongue out of a living blue whale are acting from a place of detachment from the blue whale. Detachment is not love. Therefore, I would say it is unloving.

However, a man concerned with the feeling of the animal he is about to kill, who hopes to cause the least pain and trauma, is connected. In this case I believe the kill can come within love.

If love is the glue of the universe, as with any emergent system, there will be certain ways of being that will allow individuals to ride a rising wave. If we step onto this peak, we could find our society swept along with extraordinary ease. Many things that we struggle with today would seem to melt away. Creating connections is the key.

But this is not a simplistic action, like standing still with our face to the sky expecting it to rain love. In the continuum of life, there are no absolutes. Parts of our world tend towards love or detachment. Cruelty is allowed in this world, without any doubt. Any belief system must take this into account or argue that it is all an illusion. Anyone living within this system must be prepared to defend against the deviator or we could experience the same fate as the unconditional cooperators did in the prisoner's dilemma scenario.

Free will is necessary for evolution towards love, because the ultimate goal of love is probably the creation of every kind of love possible. In order to allow everything to find love, love must first allow everything to exist. I do believe that if something becomes unloving, it will eventually die out, not because some great hand will come out of the sky and smite it, but because its very nature will lead to disconnection. If it becomes disconnected, then it's power to hold itself present will be greatly diminished. If it remains unloving, it will be like the deviant program described in the Tit For Tat scenario. Its highest possible state will be very restricted and when the peak on which it resides dips, as all peaks eventually do, it will end up much more vulnerable to extinction. It is possible that very virulent forms of disconnection are occasionally cut out by the universe, the same way we cut out cancer.

If we don't find a way to become more aware and connected, and therefore exist within a greater state of love, I believe the human race is in for a very bad time.

Because love permits the presence of cruelty does not mean that it will nurture it. I think the only way to become strong enough to withstand the presence of cruelty without being hurt ourselves is to climb the ladder love presents us in order to raise the state that our existence expresses.

It is possible that some people are in touch with these larger consciousnesses in some way and they are the ones that have brought us some amazing levels of awareness. If we allow ourselves to open up and hear what everyone is saying perhaps we could build up a picture that is far outside the ability of any one person to see.

The Choice

Every person uses the power of emergent behavior to help them along their path. The reason people tend to do as emergent behavior wishes is because there is a clear path laid out for them where help is offered. Within some systems, tremendous organizations can be built and utilitized by those people empowering that system. In economics and business, it is called capacity building. Examples of elements in society that helped everyone keep to the economic path are roads, schools, banks and government (in its current form). were defined as social capital. Social capital creates the potential for a higher peak. In the case of the economy, we were better able to create wealth because roads enabled us to transport goods more cheaply and schools trained our workers to a higher standard. Social capital is made available to any individual so we all could get better at making wealth.

The economic system is constantly creating new ways and better ways for individuals to make wealth. It empowers people who enroll in this emergent system to create far more wealth than they could possibly dream of on their own. People who are not suited or welcome into these processes have a very hard time.

Anyone who has ever lived alone in the wilderness without any tools or help will be glad to explain just how much hard work it really is. But don't confuse this with entire communities living naturally. As soon as enough people become involved in anything, some form of emergent behavior will form and capacity building will take place, making it easier for everyone. With more awareness, we can better guide the nature of the system that forms.

All emergent systems create aids to further their task. For those in science the system makes universities, microscopes and scientific journals readily available so that research is made much easier. A Muslim has access to mosques, the Qu'ran, Imams, and the Muslim community, all freely working to support the journey to becoming a better Muslim. Our bodies use the stored capacity of evolution to bring us advanced features like eyes, lungs, and bipedal motion.

In the world there many emergent systems that people can choose to align with. Frequently, we use several. Pretty much everyone in the world uses the free market system to aid their ability to buy goods and services. However, the street gangs in Miami use an emergent system to measure their lifetime success that is different from that used by monks in the Himalayas. Both groups are climbing their respective peaks but they are using a completely different emergent system to propel them upwards.

It would be short-sighted for us to judge the emergent social system used by the street gangs. What the gangs' emergent system offers that is missing in the society around them are tight bonds to other people. It is an attempt to connect in a society that is pressuring people to loosen their connections in order to be free to create as much wealth as possible. As ugly as the result is, these gang systems are filling a gap that the main social economic system is failing to provide. The measure of the ugliness is a reflection of the depth of human need being bypassed by the dominant social emergent system.

The economic system has a prime directive to make wealth, not happiness. That is why organized crime is so hard to tackle. Our economy has no interest in what people consider illegal or not. Anything that makes wealth will be empowered. That is why companies can get away with murder, why countries can slaughter animals to extinction, and why organized crime thrives. They all create wealth.

The idea of tackling the source of the drug and prostitution trade seems logical, but once again people are going to war against an emergent system. Quite frankly, it is a waste of time and money. Even if it looks successful, all that will happen is the trade will shift form and carry on.

Many of these problems can be solved by creating connections from the emergent system to whatever is important to us, just as we did earlier with rubbish. Part of my hope in this work is that people become aware enough that we can make real changes to the economic emergent system. It looks far too disconnected from the life system on earth to be allowed to continue as it is now. If we don't fix it, I believe we might find that it might suddenly unravel without much warning. This would be devastating to humankind.

There is also another way to help the situation. We could drastically reduce the influence of the economic system and relegate it to handling our material needs instead of allowing it to rule our entire lives. That would leave space for another emergent system to take its place, perhaps one that is concerned with human happiness and our connection with the other life-giving systems on earth..

There are so many systems in existence in human society that there is no way I could address even a fraction of them. But if I could suggest a guideline I would like to say that it should hold quality of life as its highest ideal. "Quality" comes from our emotions. Every single important thing in our life holds that position because of how we feel about it. We love money not because we actually have a bond with money, but because of the power it seems to give us. Once we recognize that the goal is to feel good instead of to make things that make us feel good, then we will be able to directly access what is good for us instead of using secondary methods. I am not suggesting unconscious hedonism; we must also pay attention to the nature of the peak we are aspiring to. Using these simple guidelines we could find an enormous peak.

There are some emergent systems that mould thinking of those empowering it in such a way that even perceiving the presence of an emergent systems can become very difficult. These people might repeatedly deny that they are being affected by the main emergent system in their lives. I know some very intelligent people who can see past what I have said to some very clever things that I missed, all the while remaining completely unaware of the emergent behavior I am describing. The presence of these people can be immensely frustrating, but patience is necessary. Keep in mind the importance of creating connections and bridges. As awareness continues to cascade throughout society, I believe this problem will vanish.

On the other hand, there are those that have seen or felt this their entire lives. None of what I have said is new or radical. The science I am quoting is at minimum decades old, and in some cases centuries old. We have known about emergent behavior for quite some time. We know that disconnections in society lead to problems. Faith and spirituality have for eons described emergent systems existing outside our normal awareness. All I am is the person who gathered up the pieces in one place.

Making life-giving connections is the key.

One thing that I am personally concerned about is that people in today's society have lost the ability to make connections that were as natural as breathing in previous times. Pretending not to be connected to the ecological system of the earth is a very dangerous game to play. Many people fear for the planet. I would suggest that we should fear for ourselves.

The planet and everything on it has survived colossally destructive events. When all the land on earth collided into one super continent called Pangaea, the resulting intensely hot super desert killed off 90% of all known species on earth. Did you know that it was our genetic ancestors that were among the first to bounce back when the continent broke apart and the deserts disappeared? We even enjoyed a considerable time without any significant predators. We reigned supreme until the dinosaurs evolved the trick of walking on two legs. Without a similar ability, we were moved back to survive in the shadows.

If humankind precipitates a large extinction event, we will likely suffer as much as any species. If you think our intelligence will save us, how long could most people survive in a technology-free wilderness that has been swept clean of food and fuel by our economy? This is something every other adult animal on the earth can accomplish on a daily basis. Quite frankly, if we don't find a way to connect I think our future looks very bleak. From what I can see, it looks as though humankind is approaching a crossroads and the decision we will soon make could reverberate far into our future.

Evolution has a way of finding various paths to useful items. For example, there are five or six different types of eyes that have evolved from entirely different bases. The same thing has occurred with several other useful pieces of biological gear. However, I am unaware of any other species in all this time evolving the self-awareness we have. It is potentially a tremendous gift for all the earth and it would be a shame to have it snuffed out so soon.

On the other hand, we could choose to reconnect to everyone and everything, just as we were designed to do. We could become the self-aware part of the Gaia emergent system. Perhaps we could nurture other species to avoid the same problems we are now tackling. We could become the earth's Great Barrier Reef, the consciousness that nurtures the delight of life all over the planet.

As it is written, perhaps we could take our place as a loving custodian to the earth.

The first step is recognizing how emergent behavior affects us right now. Then we have to determine what is really important to us (especially since we know that happiness is not directly linked with money). Then we find ways of connecting our society's system to these things. Next, we seek out higher states and look for what connections are necessary for emergent behavior to encourage life, love and happiness. Then we sit back and let the magic happen.

If we have the courage to look at our current problems in the face and deal with them, we could go on to inhabit a reality that so many people have sensed is possible and that is so clearly not here now.

What say you?

An Individual Journey

When I thought about writing what an individual could effectively do to bring about change, I realized that there was little that could be said without limiting personal reality. As people become more familiar with emergent behavior, I think individual paths will automatically present themselves and open up possibilities that are outside the ability of any one person to foresee.

However, there is one individual journey that I can write about without misinterpreting a life; my own. In order to keep this as short as possible, I have tried to stick only to elements that specifically relate to my developing awareness of emergent behavior.

All my adult life I have sensed that the economic system did not have my best interests at heart, but I could not understand why. As the unhappy result, even though I repeatedly tried to do the "right" thing, I always fell away. As the feeling grew, I put more effort into trying to make my own way. To the economic system, I was just noise and have been most of my life. As such, it does not support me.

As many people in this situation do, I spent a lot of time in small communities trying to avoid the critical number of people that activates certain kinds of human emergent behavior. Because small town people are less impacted by certain kinds of emergent behavior, they tend to notice and wonder about the strange behavior of big city people who are more affected by it. A frequently heard lament is that city people lack "common sense".

On the other hand, those who understand the peculiar needs of the emergent systems that we all rely on tend to see small town people as somewhat ignorant and backwards.

One of the functions of emergent behavior is to empower people to do its will. Stepping outside the helpful hand of emergent behavior is not easy. I couldn't get a loan when I had a traditional job because I have moved too many times, and I can't get one now because I don't have a traditional job. None of this measures whether I can actually pay back the loan or not. I have fallen through a crack. But I am a trained economist. I know that one has to set global policies in order to maximize efficiency, and this always results in cracks. If I put myself in the position of a large bank, I would do the same thing.

Because of my work history, I can't get a job except as the most menial worker. It is not because I am incapable or unreliable. I even have a university degree. It matters not to those who hire. They see no approved direction in my life. It is an indicator that I don't think in the proper way. They don't want to admit a noisy element in their well-oiled machine. In England, I did manage to slip through their defenses and ended up as a warehouse picker at for a large grocer. However, after I quit to take care of my dying grandmother, they would not re-hire me even though I had a spotless history as a warehouse picker.

My life could be a documentary of how to find cracks and fall into them. It has been very wearing. I wondered many times why even with all the acknowledged societal advantages, a well-educated white male from the dominant society in the world, everything was so difficult for me. I felt like a car with a good engine but no transmission to get the power to the ground.

It took pretty much all my life to convert my frustration into awareness, but now I feel have a large part of the answer. This is a synopsis of how I developed a conscious recognition of emergent behavior in humankind.

I was born in England and after a few happy years of being well ensconced in the bosom of English emergent behavior, we moved to London, Canada. Even though Canada and England look very similar, their cultural emergent behavior were completely different at the time. For example, both my parents claimed it was years before they realized Canadians had a sense of humor. Also, we landed in an area that hated the English. A motorcycle gang came and churned up our front lawn as they shouted hatred at my family and demanded that we leave. I was bullied at my first school verbally by my teacher and physically by the students. I hated Canada. I came down with terrible allergies and the doctors decided my tonsils needed to come out. Luckily, it has been the only part of my body sacrificed to the belief box of the medical profession.

All this conspired for me to pull right away from the society. Soon, I found myself studying it from the outside.

One neighbor did play with me. He claimed he was the strongest person in the world. He pointed to a rock of a size that I knew I could lift and said it was the heaviest rock in the world and only he could lift it. I didn't believe him. However, he insisted. Being only five, it didn't take many iterations of insistence to make me begin to mistrust my assessment. Still, I mustered the courage to challenge him. I suggested that I lift the stone myself. That would prove the point one way or another wouldn't it? He said that I would die if I tried.

Now, at this point, I cried and ran to my mother. But even while crying there was a part of me which kept assuring me that I would not die if I touched the rock. When my mother confirmed the I would, indeed, not die by attempting to lift a rock, I noted the part of me that had sensed the truth and I began to look for it.

A few months later, I challenged my parents about Santa Claus. Their explanations weren't adding up. Eventually, I forced them to admit that there was no Santa Claus. While I was pleased that I had worked it out on my own, I wondered why they lied like that. Why was it important not to tell my sister? Did grown-ups really see the world that much differently than I did?

Both my parents were, at the time, atheists and quite knowledgeable. The weekly reading was *New Scientist* and later on, *New Psychologist*. We were a very "intellectual" family. So it was a bit of a surprise when my parents decided that my sister and I needed to be educated in the "dominant religion".

Off to Sunday school we went. It was unbelievably boring to me. Staying awake became the Sunday torture. We begged and pleaded and played sick; anything to escape the weekly horror.

However, in spite of this we came to Believe. The people in church explained God and prayer and I immediately swung into action. I prayed to be turned into the road runner from a cartoon I loved at the time. After several days, nothing happened. I began to question what I had been learning. My prayer didn't work so either the priests were wrong or God didn't care about me. Time for a little experiment.

Being only about seven years old, it was not very sophisticated. I went out into the hall, raised my face up to God and said "Shit, God!" and ran under the sheets of my bed to protect myself from any possible lightning. None came. I tried again. Still nothing. Then I let fly with every swear word I knew. There I was standing in the hall swearing at God with a feeling of growing wonder that nothing was happening.

I thought perhaps God's anger would obliterate half of Canada when I finally told him to fuck off. So when nothing happened, especially after all that I had been told at Sunday school, I started to wonder whether God really existed. I knew prayer didn't work and He obviously didn't respond to sin (what could possibly be more sinful than using the "f" word?), so even if He did exist, what was the point?

At about the same time, the Church showed us a double exposure and claimed it was an angel. My father went ballistic (for him, he was quite reserved, really). He explained to us how double exposures worked, how the church was speaking rubbish, and that ended the Sunday school experiment. In hindsight, I wonder if it was simply a way for our parents to be rid of us on Sunday mornings.

I stopped believing in Christianity.

Challenging beliefs was an early exercise for me. I was quite surprised when I later found myself so completely ensnared in one.

It was soon after that I began to recognize patterns in my social system. I was totally in love with a girl at school but it was really hard to connect with girls at my young age. So I was astonished when this girl started to walk home with me. However, I knew from observation that the social cycle of the seven year-olds at my school was about six weeks. I told her that in six weeks, instead of being my friend she would be throwing abuse at me from a different group. She told me I was full of rubbish (in a sweet Canadian way). Guess what? Six weeks later she was yelling taunts at me from her new group of friends.

School was becoming as painful as Sunday school had been. To this day, I dread being forced to sit in apparent attention while feeling like my brains are dribbling out of my head. I hated boredom. Why, I wondered, do they do it this way when everyone is bored? Is there some hidden benefit of boring someone to insensibility that I was too childish to notice? I saw adults doing the same thing to themselves with their "meetings". I wondered whether the world was mad. But I realized I was likely wrong because adults, who ran the world, were far smarter than I was. I wanted to get older so I would understand.

During my school days, emergent behavior tried to shift me into the groove of misfit. But I had already developed an instinctive, but unconscious, skill of stepping outside the influence of the unhelpful aspects of emergent systems. In this case, I simply did not accept the label I was given. It wasn't something I had to struggle with, it just fell off me. I didn't have access to the emergent behavior's benefits of being popular, but neither was I victimized.

By the age of twelve, my fellow students nicknamed me Dim Tim because rarely could I answer questions correctly in class. To me, the whole process of school was becoming an absurd exercise in keeping young people off the streets while killing off any desire to explore and question the world. It seemed to me that school was pre-packaging what was important, telling us what history meant, and teaching us how to slot ourselves neatly into the machinery of society. I realize now that this attitude was an unconscious rejection of emergent system. At the time, it seemed to me that the school system was more intent on conditioning children to become effective workers, and was not in the least bit interested in helping anyone increase their awareness.

Rather astonishingly, I managed to graduate from high school, though my grades were just above a certain critical point.

Freedom at last, but I soon discovered that a relatively uneducated freedom was difficult. My social ineptitude combined with an unfortunate intellectual arrogance did not make me very employable. I failed an IQ entrance test for management training. Even McDonalds would not hire me. This was not an auspicious start to my working life.

It is also what happens to people when they step outside the empowering grasp of emergent behavior.

Eventually, I decided that I needed to shore up some personal weaknesses. The years of emphasizing science and logic combined with limited social interaction left me incompetent in society. I was agonizingly shy of doing anything in front of anyone and I was tired of feeling this way.

After walking past their door several times, I finally managed to force myself to apply to the ballroom dance instructor training program being advertised by Fred Astaire Dance Studios. Not surprisingly, it did not go smoothly. I was sacked once in training and twice after successfully completing their courses. Each time I was sacked, like a bad cold, I kept finding ways to return. However, I was still failing on all recognizable levels.

After a huge amount of work I finally managed to eek out an existence as a dance instructor. It was here that I was exposed to some of the best sales motivators in the world. The way they looked at the world was fascinating. They introduced me to a book called *The Greatest Salesman on Earth* by Og Mandino which shifted the way I looked at many things and was a key factor in enabling me to become very successful as a dance instructor.

After a painful ending, I returned home to become a dead meat butcher. Dead meat means the animal dies away from the slaughter house, frequently from natural causes. But I learned a lot about anatomy and was even entrusted with the occasional autopsy. I also became very strong in both physical strength and smell. But it was mainly boring work and I needed to find a different path.

My mother had found spirituality. It took a while to solidify, but after deeply researching every channeled book she could get her hands on she eventually settled in something called Right Use of Will. I went through the same journey with her because she did the best thing of all to engage me; she asked me which one I felt was the most valid. My considerable conceit was engaged and I jumped in determined to effectively evaluate all the different systems.

One of the beliefs that was on offer was that whatever people believed would be their reality. But if this was true then how did different people's beliefs interact to shape everything? This sent my mind to trying to conceive how everybody working together would shape the world.

This idea, and many others, woke me out of my slumber. It spoke to my feeling of being different and my sense that I could see things that others couldn't. After many years of indoctrination by my mother, I finally became a spiritual being. She dragged the whole family off to a workshop given by the author of Right Use of Will and there I found a subtle sense of mystery, awe, and hidden knowledge that could unlock magical powers. It seemed like the fantasy books that I liked to read were coming true in reality. I was absolutely hooked.

Spirituality has a well-developed belief system with a complex, interesting, and challenging logical structure which could take years to explore. I got a Reiki degree and started working on my karma. Growth was the goal, emotional pain the symptom and emotional expression the tool; I would be healed!

I was surrounded by hundreds of people evolving and growing and explaining in credible terms their increasing awareness and presence, sweeping me along in euphoria that the magical world we all wanted would soon be manifest. However, the part of my mind that questioned whether lifting the rock would actually kill me stirred and began marking things for further testing when the opportunity arose.

Four years after I left high school I went to university. My mother channeled the fact that a daughter of one of her friends was my soulmate. She had been accepted by York University. Off I went. I never did meet that soulmate.

Originally, I had planned to get a business degree, but that changed when I took my first economics course. I was fascinated by this way of looking at society. Whereas in high school I barely scraped by with minimum marks, whereas I had failed an IQ test, suddenly I was in the top four percent of the entire university.

During that summer, a friend of mine invited me down to meet some sexy girls attending his university. We let them ride our motorcycles in a car park with us on the back making sure nothing went wrong. I noticed that my girl was steering very close to a curb in her lazy loops around the lot but I decided she must have noticed and I should not bother her.

After several safe circuits, she hit the curb.

We were only doing about 7 mph but the force was just right to bend a lot of bits on my bike. I repaired my beloved bike as much as I could afford. Unfortunately, the bike was now quite unpleasant to ride. I fantasized about having someone crash into my bike so I could collect the insurance and buy a better bike. As a spiritualist I believed that reality stems from our thoughts and beliefs so what happened next should not have been a surprise. While stationary in a queue, I was rear-ended by a van doing over 50 miles per hour.

It messed up my back (hurts to this day) and scrambled my ability to concentrate. My marks at university plummeted. However, with the insurance, I bought my first superbike.

To me, this was a clear demonstration that thoughts really do manifest reality. My belief strengthened.

In school, my enthusiasm for economics waned. I started to sense something deeper. I couldn't quite put my finger on it but I took a stab at objectively describing my feelings by writing a paper called the Disutility of Neo-classical Economics. The paper got a B and the truth is that was probably a bit generous.

A couple of years after I graduated I ended up in the Yukon Territory and became the Economic Development Officer for the Little Salmon/Carmacks First Nation. I still hate trying to write that title in the tiny space designated in job application forms. Basically, what this meant was that I was in charge of the policies that would lead a Native American community into the market economy. Fertile ground indeed.

Living among the Native Americans showed me first hand the damage sustained by their society. They had endured the destruction of their culture and their resources, forced abduction and education of their children. The stated purpose of these resident schools was to re-educated the Native Americans as mainstream people. However, the children were subjected to numerous forms of mass abuse of all types, including sexual.

The result was heartbreaking. Alcoholism was rife. Native Americans are genetically more susceptible to alcoholism than Europeans and it devastated their communities. The returning sexual abuse victims did not always win their fight with the resulting demons, especially when alcohol took advantage of their battered sense of self. Sexual abuse then appeared within their community. Unemployment was chronic. The connection of productivity and earnings was frequently absent. This was the raw material that the "city people" were now demanding be hammered into an effective capitalistic community within five years.

For anyone on the ground, healing the people was the main priority. Many healing techniques were being tried in these communities. Tens of thousands of dollars were being spent on traditional healing camps, self-improvement seminars, psychology, counseling and just about anything else you could think of. It was a huge effort that yielded only marginal and frequently temporary improvements.

At this time I was rabidly anti-religious. Organized religions' involvement in the destruction of the Native American culture and its documented sexual abuse of hundreds of children fuelled this to a fever pitch. I hated the church and everything it represented. I felt part of my role was to unbrainwash anyone who seemed vulnerable to falling into this dark unsavory world.

I was speaking to one of the elders of this community and she was telling me about her struggle with alcohol. It had stolen much of her adulthood. I was quite surprised because I had never seen her drink. Constantly trying to find effective ways to heal my adopted community, I asked her how she got off the alcohol.

"I found Jesus and he gave me the strength."

I must have gaped. All this effort and money gone into complex healing schemes and one little belief was all it had taken for this woman.

It forced me to reconsider just how purely evil the church was. The most obvious sign was that a lot of the Native Americans had fiercely embraced Christianity. It must have been giving something back. This was the beginning of the end of my prejudice towards Christians.

One of the great things about the Yukon is that nature is still the dominant force there. There was a sea of natural life and with only little islands comprised of people. This allowed me to be around what I considered to be natural animal behavior.

One day I looked out of my office to see a small bird caught in a fishing net. It was flapping frantically in an impossible tangle so I went out to rescue it. At first it pecked at me in frantic desperation, but it was too small to hurt me much. I carefully unwrapped the bird. The untangling process slowed down even more when I noticed the bird's wing had been cut to the bone.

By the time I had freed it, it was sitting calmly on my finger. I raised my hand to a tree to give it a high perch, but it decided to stay on my finger. So, I went back into my office and worked for another half an hour on my computer, one-handed of course, because the other hand had a bird on it. After some time, I decided to try to get the bird into a tree again. Halfway to the tree, the bird jumped and tried to fly but couldn't maintain height and ended up on the ground. There were several cats that lived in the area and I was worried for the bird so I slowly approached to lift it to a branch. The bird panicked as it backed under a structure too small for me to follow.

Now, I was in a quandary. Do I try jumping on the bird to recapture it and risk possibly injuring it or frightening it to death, or do I leave it to its destiny?

I pondered the situation. I noticed the bird's natural makeup was not correctly interpreting the situation. It was running on its normal programming that kept the species as a whole alive (don't present yourself to a possible predator) but that same programming would probably doom this individual bird. I wondered if people did the same thing.

During this time, I became very active in my spirituality. The people I was working with would meet periodically and some of them would later become my closest friends. We were working on the principle that human beings were spiritual beings who need to clear up judgment and denied emotions in order to heal our bodies and raise the consciousness of everything. Since most of the people from my group lived in the United States, my focus shifted south.

I decided to close up my life in the Yukon. I had just finished tidying up all the loose ends, walked into my home and said to a friend, "I wonder what I am going to do now?"

Immediately, the telephone rang. It was a Right Use of Will person from Denver, wondering if I could come down and work with them because I kept coming up in their healing. These people, who I barely knew, were part of the "core group". The invitation was a rare gift to someone of my belief. I looked at my friend in astonishment. Well, actually we stared at each other in the smug knowledge that our belief was the Truth.

The final pieces were in place. My interpretation of this belief rapidly evolved.

I spent several weeks with these people before landing in Santa Fe, New Mexico and marrying a girl I had met in the group.

But outside the world of my group, things were not going well. As with most beliefs, things not going well had to be interpreted as me not applying my belief with either the wisdom or fervor required. I decided to throw myself into healing as fast as I could. This meant that I was opening myself up to immense emotional pain. I braced myself.

First, my marriage broke up. Then, continuing unsettling patterns within the group finally made me decide I had to put some distance between myself and all my closest friends. As much as this was the right decision, this effectively cut me off from all but a couple of my closest friends.

On hearing of my marriage break-up, a woman in England told me she was my soulmate and had been waiting forever (many reincarnations through all of time) for me to notice. I was quite vulnerable to this because my mother had brought me up to believe that women were far more insightful and aware than men, especially around feelings. It was the men who blundered in with crude sexual desires destroying any love that could have been possible. Women knew feelings and didn't I realize that feelings were the root of all of creation? Who should be listened to then? I was simply part of the army of men that made women miserable and there were several very miserable women around me at that time.

In spite of serious misgivings, I decided I must follow my feelings and face my fate like a man. I moved back to England to live with my soulmate. I was thrown out within a few weeks. I was left with no job, no money and no legal means of immediately acquiring either. I ended up sleeping on the living room floor in a tiny flat of my ex soulmate's friend.

I had lost everything. I was very close to my breaking point.

At the time, I believed that in order for a belief to be valid, it had to contain all of reality. I began to see bits of reality that my belief system didn't explain. All the niggly little things I had been noting all along suddenly came forward in a cascade of doubt. But if I turned my back on this loving God and all the healing, would I be turning my back on all life, as my belief system said I would? Then I realized, if He was really there and loving, He would understand.

I finally picked up the rock and I did not die.

But I almost did.

Stepping out of a fully formed mature adult belief system is not like discovering Santa Claus is not real. It would be wise for any adult contemplating jettisoning their beliefs to make sure they have vast reserves of support. I was weak and practically alone—I became very suicidal.

This was the darkest period of my life.

For a few weeks, my life hung on daily phone calls to a friend and my ex-wife. They saved my life.

As my emotional turmoil turned me inside out, I noticed something that I thought was extraordinary. Some days I felt okay. The reason this was so extraordinary was that nothing in reality had changed.

Most of the time I wallowed in emotional agony, just trying to make it through each single day. I had always said that if my belief was wrong I would rather die. There was nothing in the world for me that I could see. Then, quite strangely, on small islands of time, I felt quite content to live. How can this be? All the things that were causing me such pain were still present and yet my emotional response was vastly different. Especially coming from a belief that said emotions were reality, this was a real revelation.

Then I wondered; if my belief is wrong, what belief is right? How can I know that it is right? I certainly didn't want to go through this pain again.

So I tried to look reality square in the face but ran into a problem. There was too much reality out there. Without a belief system to filter and sort information, I was being completely overwhelmed. I couldn't retain even a fraction of the information flowing over me from life. I'm not talking about television, books or internet. What I would do was sit in a chair and simply let in all the noises and detail and events that were going on around me. The massive amount of information would quickly fill my brain. The better I got at opening myself up the faster my brain would fill. It got so I could look out at reality and within seconds I would simply fill up. It was then I realized one of the purposes of belief systems was to filter reality so our brains could function.

I began to write down my thoughts with the intent of constructing my own belief system using proven reality. Then I noticed just how tenuous is our individual perception. All of us experience things in our own way. Some of the most heated arguments occur when two people experience the same occurrence and come away with two totally different perceptions of what happened. Both have absolute certainty that their version of reality is right and the fight begins.

It was then I wondered if science was the answer. I dived back into science books and acquainted myself with the latest understandings available to non-scientists. Science had moved a long way since I had last taken a good look but, like economics, it left me with a feeling that something was missing.

Then it dawned on me. If one belief could not contain reality then perhaps all the beliefs together could see the unseeable. Perhaps it could even create a state change in the human consciousness. I began to unravel how reality might be if we all accepted each others' beliefs and worked from there. It was a glorious vision.

With this picture dancing in my mind, I called friends to share to share my excitement. As I reached for different ways to relate this picture, I found myself without any way to communicate it. The frustration was indescribable.

I retreated in order to search for a way to lead my friends to what I saw. The key problem was that there were elements of this picture that lay outside my friends' beliefs. The more I studied this the larger and more impassable the barrier seemed. In order to share my vision I had to get my friends to see something that they did not believe could be true. How could I approach them on equal ground and pry open their belief without triggering a defensive barrage? If they refused, either consciously or unconsciously, there would be no way from me to relate what I saw.

And even if I could, should I? A person's belief is a very sensitive thing. What if I unintentionally hurt people, as I had in the past?

But the potential of the vision drove me forward. I decided that I should at least try, as gently as I could.

Since I was studying my friends' beliefs, I thought I might as well have a look at how one might open up all peoples' beliefs. After agonizing on ways to talk to all people from all beliefs, my conclusion was it is not possible. The larger the number of beliefs simultaneously addressed the less reality will be universally accepted. If someone tries to speak credibly to every belief on earth, there is nothing left to be said.

This process led me to form the concept of the belief box. I decided that no one would be able to engage with the "big picture" until they were aware of how their own beliefs determined how the world was experienced. So I wrote *Beyond Belief.* I had hoped that it was all that would be needed to trigger a shift and people would find their own way to their own version of the "picture" I saw.

It utterly failed. Even people who had known me for decades had no idea of what I was on about.

I retreated. Perhaps I didn't have all the necessary elements to be successful in getting these ideas out into the public. Some other people must be seeing what I am seeing and perhaps one of these people would be better able to communicate with the public consciousness.

I spent another couple of years trying to be "normal" before the pressures finally built up again. Ignoring some rather unsettling trends in my bank account, I dropped everything I had been doing and wrote down a path directly leading to this vision as clearly as I could. People would either find a way to deal with their belief boxes or not. It was up to them.

The result sits in your hands.

Final Thoughts

My big dream is that this becomes the beginning of a discussion that will lead to profound life-giving connections across the world. There is so much to say that each of the different chapters could easily be expanded into a book in its own right. I have tried to keep my descriptions at a minimum because the more I describe my own vision, the less room reality has to freely express itself. The potential of our unified vision is directly related to the freedom people have to express what they see. After that, it becomes a process of connecting, learning, evolving, and understanding.

There are two main fears for a writer of this kind of work. One is that the work will be ignored. If this happens it will affect no one but me. But the second concern is people take it too seriously. Just as a precaution, I would like to say that if anyone uses something in this book as a weapon or means for disconnection, then they have not understood the main points. In fact, the potential for gentle connection is a good measure of how effective a proposed action might be.

Having said that, I would like to impose one thought. One of the key nodal points in human society is the experience of our children and young adults. If we want to even touch the potential of humankind we need to create a society that generates a joyful expansive experience for our children and fully supports our young adults as they search for a peak to which to aspire.

It is frequently said that children are extremely resilient. However, existing and living are too completely different states. I was never abused as a child and still I was nearly forty before I could overcome some rather unfortunate conditioning I took on as a child. Every year spent working with my conditioning could have been used instead to build a meaningful life. Some childhood trauma or programming can haunt the resulting adult for their entire lives. Unless it is resolved, adults then visit their trauma, at some level, on almost every people they meet. Traumas become multiplied throughout society until they become huge problems.

Happy people do not commit rape and genocide, abuse children, or need prove how tough they are, or fly airplanes into office buildings.

This is a vast untapped potential that is currently wilting on the barren ground of our current emergent system. Every generation that grows up bearing scars from childhood dramatically reduces the potential that is possible for human-kind. With feedback, this has magnified until war, murder, and criminal gangs have become not only accepted, but expected as a given of the human condition. In fact, I would wager that there are a number of readers who simply do not belief that we could create a society without the presence of these social ills. That is the power of emergent behavior in action.

It does not have to be this way.

This is not an indictment of individual parents. With rare exceptions, parents do the best they can considering what burdens they are carrying. Our society is currently programmed to maximize wealth. Everything is bent to that goal. Children are expenses, not wealth. As such, they are not really valued by the emergent behavior of society until they become wage earners. The only value they have is measured by whatever money the parents are willing to spend on their behalf. This is one reason why the children of the rich frequently do so much better. They feel a sense of value from society. Poor children grow up frequently feeling like they are unwanted burdens, except where they are put to work as child labor-ers, which creates different scars. This is not necessarily because their parents are unloving, but because emergent behavior of our society is.

This problem has become so bad that "noise" has arisen in society in the form of charities trying to protect children from all manner of ills. Within these orga-nizations lie some of society's most potent wisdom.

If we decide to tackle only one nodal point, this one would be my suggestion. Just as trauma can multiply into a frightening societal disease, like suicide bomb-ings, a growing presence of joy could just as easily explode into a world-wide epi-demic.

However, if we can find the willpower to understand and tackle just a few more key issues on earth today, we have a very real chance of making changes that might seem magical to people who do not understand emergent behavior. It breaks my heart to see society make so many decisions that will perpetuate misery for so many, sometimes for generations to come.

If we keep on doing what we are doing then, except by catastrophe, the world will not significantly change. If we accept that we need to change then it is a mat-ter of finding a better path. I hope the information in the book demonstrates that the path is not only available in reality, but we can begin to access it right now.

Of course, having a few individuals change direction will do little in the immediate future. However, because systems adhere to the rule of sensitive initial conditions, over time, the effort of every single person has the potential to significantly change the direction of society in the future.

There is even a possibility that you are a key nodal point in the process of bringing consciousness back to society. You don't necessarily have to be rich or powerful, you just have to be the right person in the right place. You will never know unless you try. In fact, the willingness to try is one of the few necessary characteristics of anyone capable of great deeds.

If enough people become aware of emergent behavior and its unseen role in our lives, there is a real possibility that what would be considered a miracle today might become a reality much sooner than we can imagine.

Our own awareness is the easiest thing to shift in the first instance. Once this occurs, true change will be within our grasp.

I am hoping to find people who feel we have waited long enough. Change could happen quickly if we decide that is it finally time.

Books I Found Interesting

Ronald Wright, *Stolen Continents*, (Viking Penguin, New York, 1992)

This is a study of how history progressed from 1492 onwards from the Native American point of view. This book gives a good sense of the immense tragedy that the Native Americans felt as their civilizations were destroyed over the last 500 years.

John Gribbin, *Deep Simplicity*, (Penguin, USA, 2005)
Philip Ball, *Critical Mass*, (Heinemann, United Kingdom, 2004)
Steven Johnson, *Emergence*, (Scribner, USA, 2001)

These three books are recent popular science books tackling the subject of emergent behavior. They all contain interesting studies and facts that have emerged from the latest research in the fields of emergent behavior, complexity and chaos.

Robert Axelrod and Michael D Cohen, *Harnessing Complexity*, (The Free Press, USA, 1999)

This is a clear summation of the scientific view of complexity. It lays out all the components of emergent systems, names them, and demonstrates how they work. Quite a dry read.

James Gleick, *Chaos*, (Viking Penguin, USA, 1987)

This is the hugely popular book that started it all for many non-scientists. It opens up the entire field of chaos for an inquiring reader. There are lots of relevant illustrations and individual stories that keep the story interesting. It's worth reading a larger version as some of the illustrations are incredibly complex and beautiful.

Ziauddin Sardar and Iwona Abrams, *Introducing Chaos*, (Totem Books, USA, 1999)
J.P. McEvoy and Oscar Zarate, *Introducing Quantum Theory*, (Totem Books, USA, 1999)

These "Introducing…" books are like comic books for wannabe scientists. They are full of irreverent humor but are masters of taking difficult concepts and making them simple and accessible. There are a number of "Introducing…" titles for those who might be interested.

Arie de Geus, *The Living Company*, (Nicholas Brealey, United Kingdom, 1997)

This is a fascinating journey taken by a retired director of Shell/Royal Dutch. The initial impetus was an internal Shell study that the average lifespan of a Fortune 500 was only 40-50 years. De Geus went on to identify and study the characteristics that differentiated the very long-lived corporations from normal corporations. They will be quite surprising for some. His vast experience in Shell led him to recognize key nodal points in the business model and outline several methods of reprogramming business to create enormous benefits for shareholders and society alike. As far as I can tell, he does this without any specific knowledge emergent systems.

Stephen Hawking with Leonard Mlodinow, *A Briefer History of Time*, (Bantam Press, London, 2005)

This is an overview of how physicists view time. Quite readable and the hardback version has pretty drawings in it.

Richard Dawkins, *The Ancestor's Tale*, (Weidenfeld and Nicolson, United Kingdom, 2005)

This is his latest book in his never-ending promotion of the scientific view of evolution which began with *The Selfish Gene*. This book is particularly interesting because he traces humankind's genetic evolution as far back in time as the limits of science permit. There are some fascinating facts in this book.

Callum Coats, *Living Energies*, (Gateway Books, UK, 1996)

This is a summation of the work done by Viktor Schauberger, a practical scientist that did most of his work with what he called natural energies. Though he examined many natural processes, the bulk of his work was with water and air flows and resulted in many unorthodox conclusions. He was proven right a number of times in the face of established opposition, so even if some of his work was a bit fanciful (over-unity engines, for example), I think he is worth a look, especially for those interested in healthy natural processes.

Jane Roberts, *Seth Speaks: The Eternal Validity of the Soul*, (Amber-Allen Publishing, US, June 1994)

If you want to get a taste of the subtle complexity of spirituality, this is the book that hooked me twenty years ago. Other than that, I am a little reluctant to recommend spiritual books because they rarely build on each other. From my point of view, many of the authors are trying to describe benefits of a particular peak that they have found. This is quite similar to self-help books. Like shoes, fitting oneself to these peaks is a very personal thing. I would suggest to anyone newly interested to browse the personal growth/spirituality section of their local bookshop. Or do a internet search.

978-0-595-40653-1
0-595-40653-X

www.ingramcontent.com/pod-product-compliance
Lightning Source LLC
Chambersburg PA
CBHW020442290526
45785CB00002B/971